Kirsty Manning-Wilcox and Pe...

Photography by Jacqui Henshaw

We Love Food
Family recipes from the garden

Kirsty
For Alex, Henry, Jemima and Charlie with love.

Peta
For John and Barb Heine for igniting my passion for food
and teaching me that commitment is everything.

hardie grant books
MELBOURNE · LONDON

Contents

Introduction

We Love Food is for families who want a simple, practical and achievable way to create and celebrate food – in the garden and on the table. We believe cooking, gardening, harvesting, preparing and sharing food is integral to family life and will lay the foundations for a lifetime appreciation of food.

We Love Food focuses on eating fruit and vegetables in season. Not only do fruit and vegetables taste their best when in season, they're also cheaper – and it makes sense to eat food that is grown locally, rather than imported out of season. Just because you can buy strawberries in winter doesn't mean you should!

Growing and buying your produce in season means your family can look forward to certain foods at different times of the year. Who doesn't love the onset of summer and its oodles of berries and mangoes, or the anticipation of minestrone soup bursting with flavour in autumn and winter? Spending time in the garden will help your children understand the cycle of life. Not only will they be harvesting their own vegetables, they will see them go from the basket to the kitchen and onto the table for dinner. But don't worry if you don't have a vegetable garden – head to your local farmers' market and let the kids look and taste the array of fresh fruit and vegetables on display.

There's no need to be precious about our recipes – many of the ingredients can be swapped to match whatever is in your garden, fridge or cupboard, and we encourage you to make these recipes your own. Like the gardening tips, the recipes are simple and quick, and we have geared the chapters to match the demands of a busy family life. There are weeknight dinners for staples, soups to have as a backup, salads and vegetables to spice up any meal, and slow cooking and more elaborate dishes for the weekend when there's time to shop, prepare and entertain. We've even got some breakfast ideas in here to break the monotonous cereal cycle. For inspiration and smooth sailing during the week, check out the kids' lunchbox chapter for delicious healthy snacks that won't float around at the bottom of the school bag! Lastly, we have some sweet treats for the whole family and a section of pickles, relishes and preserves so you can extend the magic of every season in your pantry.

Throughout the book, we've included some of our SOS recipe ideas – these are our top tips to get food on the table when time is short and tummies are grumbling.

We've also included basic guidelines on how to grow some of our favourite fruit and vegetables – staples like tomatoes, lettuce, potatoes, peas and beans, and sweet treats like strawberries and rhubarb – as this helps kids understand that food is a soil to table process. It need not matter whether your garden is a few pots with lettuce, herbs and cherry tomatoes or a full-scale kitchen garden. Including kids in the process creates a sense of achievement that will positively influence their relationship with food far more than dinner table bribes or threats ever will.

Eat together as often as you can to encourage your kids by example. By eating with your children you can create a conversation about food. This conversation can begin in the garden and the kitchen. If you are preparing a fruit salad and have a beautiful melon, encourage them to smell it and comment. This involvement in the food before it reaches the table gives your child confidence and you will often find their natural curiosity overrides their reason for not trying a particular dish or ingredient.

Taste is not always the reason kids refuse to try something – it can often be the way it looks or smells. As a parent, you need to think of ways to involve all their senses so they are not ruled by just one. For example, if your child won't taste, then at least get them to smell the food and tell you what they think.

We are not suggesting that you go through this process for every meal, but in our experience these strategies work well over time and with patience. So, above all, keep trying. As with all new experiences with children, whether it be riding a bike, learning to read or trying new flavours, repetition and praise are the keys to success.

Breakfasts

Let's face it:
during the week cereal,
toast, fruit and yoghurt are the breakfast
staples on busy mornings. Between preparing
school lunches, locating homework and sporting
equipment, and packing school bags, there
isn't much time for anything else.

However, if you're looking to break
the monotony of weekday breakfasts
try the Moroccan Breakfast
Couscous, Banana and
Cinnamon Porridge
or make a batch of Sweet
Lemon Pikelets and pop
a couple in the lunchbox
as a special treat.

If you're planning brunch with
friends, or having a tribe of kids
for a sleepover, then the Fried
Asparagus Rolls and Tomato and Prosciutto
Skewers look great at the breakfast table on platters.

Enlist the help of your children to set the table.
If you have a garden, send the kids outside to pick some
flowers, fresh parsley and chives for garnishes or to stir
through scrambled eggs.

On the weekend, treat yourself and the family
by preparing something a little more elaborate.
Try an Extra Special BLT,
some Quick Baked Beans or
Creamy Scrambled Eggs.
Divvy up the weekend newspaper
and make an extra
pot of coffee.

Perfect poached eggs with tomato and prosciutto skewers

4 wooden skewers
16 cherry tomatoes, cut in half
4 slices prosciutto
freshly ground black pepper
2–3 tablespoons olive oil
1 tablespoon white vinegar
4 free-range eggs
4 slices buttered toast

Preparation time: 10 minutes
Cooking time: 10 minutes
Serves 4

This is a gorgeous breakfast in summer, when tomatoes are at their seasonal best. The secret to perfect poached eggs is using the freshest eggs available.

Soak the wooden skewers in water for 5 minutes to prevent burning during cooking. Thread one tomato half on a skewer, then weave a slice of prosciutto along the skewer, alternating with a quarter of the tomato halves. Repeat the process with the remaining skewers. Season the skewers with freshly ground black pepper and drizzle with the oil.

Half-fill a deep frying pan with water, add the vinegar and bring to a simmer over medium heat. Crack an egg into a cup. Stir the water until it becomes a whirlpool then gently tip the egg into the middle of the whirlpool. Cook for 3 minutes for a runny egg and 4 minutes for a firm egg.

Gently lift the egg out of the water with a slotted spoon and place onto a clean tea towel to soak up the excess water. Transfer to a plate and cover with a tea towel to keep warm while you poach the other eggs.

Cook the skewers on a hot char-grill pan or barbecue grill plate for 4–5 minutes, or until the prosciutto is crispy and the tomatoes have softened. Turn them a few times to achieve an even, golden effect. Remove to plates and serve with a poached egg and toast on the side.

Runny boiled eggs with fried asparagus rolls

8 asparagus spears

8 slices wholemeal bread,
   crusts removed

4 free-range eggs

olive oil

salt and freshly ground black pepper

Preparation time: 15 minutes
Cooking time: 10 minutes
Serves 4

This is a great take on eggs with toast soldiers – kids love dipping the asparagus rolls into the gooey egg. If by chance you leave the eggs cooking too long and they become hardboiled, simply turn them into egg salad for a lunchbox sandwich and start again.

Cut or break the woody ends off the asparagus spears and discard. Blanch the asparagus in boiling water for 2 minutes, or until just tender. Drain well and pat dry with paper towel.

Arrange an asparagus spear diagonally across a slice of bread, corner to corner. Fold the bread over the asparagus and carefully roll up. Give the wrapped asparagus a light squeeze with your hand to seal. Repeat with the remaining asparagus and bread.

Pour in enough oil to come 2 cm up the sides of a heavy frying pan and place over medium heat. Use the crusts you have cut off to test if the oil is hot enough – the bread should turn golden in about 15 seconds.

Add the asparagus rolls and gently sauté for 3–4 minutes, turning occasionally, until golden and crispy. Place the cooked rolls on paper towel to soak up any excess oil.

Heat a large saucepan of water over high heat. Just before the water boils, gently add the eggs. Let the water come to a rolling boil, then reduce the heat to medium so the water is just simmering and cook for 3 minutes. Gently transfer the eggs to egg cups and slice off the tops. Season with salt and freshly ground black pepper and serve with the asparagus rolls on the side.

 note

To give the dish a little more pizzazz, roll up prosciutto or shaved ham with the asparagus in the bread before cooking. If you prefer, replace the asparagus with a few green beans or a long wedge of zucchini.

SILVERBEET AND CHARD

Think of silverbeet and chard as the jeans of the vegetable world – reliable and adaptable for any occasion. For little effort you get plenty of leaves to pick over for a couple of years, which is why they're often referred to as 'cut and come again' plants.

Chard is the collective name given to the variety of green leafy vegetables related to the beetroot and spinach families. Chard varieties are generally distinguished by their stems, which come in a range of colours, including red, yellow and white, which increase in vibrancy during cool weather. Silverbeet, or Swiss chard, is the most commonly known variety of chard, with dark green leaves and a thick, creamy stem.

Silverbeet and chard are perfect for energetic families as they're packed full of iron. So, if you're feeling a little tired and run-down, try adding these glossy greens to your meals – raw in a salad, juiced for a breakfast energy hit or steamed with a drizzle of lemon juice, olive oil and freshly ground black pepper. Aside from iron, these juicy greens also contain vitamins A and C, as well as folate – a vital nutrient for pregnant women.

Soil and site

Silverbeet and chard like moist, fertile soil and need to be protected from strong sun and winds. If you live in a terrace or townhouse, the narrow strip on the sunny side is the perfect spot for these vegetables. Chard varieties thrive in salty soils – good news for all the sea-change families.

These plants tend to suck up nitrogen and potassium, so feed the soil with compost, blood and bone or poultry manure six weeks before planting. If you have prepared the soil well, you shouldn't need to fertilise regularly, but you may want to give the plants a top-up with a complete fertiliser or seaweed solution when it is coming up to the height of summer – or depths of winter – so they stay strong and healthy. Although some people recommend fertilising fortnightly, this is only necessary if you have poor soil with little or no organic matter worked into it.

Planting

Sew seeds directly into the soil in early spring, summer or autumn, or as soon as the frosts finish in your area. Silverbeet and chard are hardy plants – they'll survive the occasional frost and snow, as well as the odd heat wave.

Prior to planting, soak the seeds for 12 to 24 hours – this helps to speed up the germination process. Get the kids to help you plant the seeds in holes 5 cm deep and 25 cm apart. Once the seedlings pop through the soil you'll need to thin out the weak plants and leave 30 cm between the plants so that the large wrinkly leaves have room to grow.

If you're planting seedlings, a punnet with six to eight plants should keep most families in business throughout the year. It's a good idea to buy a couple of different chard varieties and swap half-punnets with your friends or neighbours so you can all enjoy the spectacular colour varieties of the plants.

If you like, show off your silverbeet and the gorgeous red-stemmed ruby chard as feature pot plants. Plant in deep pots, at least 50 cm deep, or half wine barrels. Use premium standard potting mix, mulch well, add water-saving crystals and water regularly to ensure the pots don't dry out.

Growing

You can companion plant silverbeet and chard with any legume apart from runner beans, as the roots of runner beans are poisonous after cutting back.

Silverbeet and chard also grow well beside onions, leafy lettuces and members of the brassica family, such as cabbage, broccoli and cauliflower. For a truly beautiful feature, plant some silverbeet or ruby chard in your herb garden alongside lavender, thyme, mint, sage and garlic.

As part of a crop-rotation cycle, we recommend planting silverbeet and chard after the soil has been enriched by nitrogen-giving legumes, such as peas, beans and alfalfa. You should also consider a follow-up crop of legumes when you remove the plants every couple of years to enrich the soil. Light-feeding plants, such as carrots, are a good crop to follow silverbeet and chard in your garden bed rotation cycle.

Pests and diseases

Silverbeet and chard can suffer from mildew (fluffy mould on the underside of the leaves), so ensure you leave about 30 cm between plants so air can circulate.

Slugs, snails and caterpillars thrive on silverbeet and chard, so get the kids to check the plants regularly and pick off the pests. Or, if you prefer, you can make your own non-toxic Chilli Spray (page 72) or Garlic Spray (page 107) to blitz the bugs.

Harvesting

It will take six to eight weeks before you can start harvesting sliverbeet and chard leaves. The leaves grow to a maximum of about 30 cm long, but you should also harvest some of the tender baby leaves to use in salads, as they are so delicious.

You need to harvest silverbeet and chard regularly, cutting the base of each leaf with scissors or a kitchen knife. Harvest the biggest leaves from the outside first. It is best to leave a few leaves on each plant to encourage regrowth.

You can adopt a 'cut and come again' approach with silverbeet and chard. If you chop leaves back to the bottom of the stem, you will encourage a set of regrowth to carry you through summer. We recommend regular harvesting to stop the plants bolting to seed early and the leaves becoming bitter and inedible.

In hot weather it's best to harvest silverbeet and chard early in the morning, otherwise the leaves tend to be too droopy. But, if you do need to revive hot and droopy leaves, wash the leaves in cold water, wrap them in a clean cloth to dry and place the cloth in the refrigerator. In about 30 minutes you'll have perfectly crispy leaves.

Quick ways with silverbeet and chard

- Young silverbeet and chard leaves are delicious and sweet, making them the perfect choice for salads.

- Steam or sauté a large bunch of leaves and add soy or tamari sauce for a simple Asian-inspired side dish. Silverbeet and chard make an excellent replacement for leafy Asian greens if you don't have any to hand.

- Add finely chopped leaves to a grilled cheese sandwich or pizza for a healthy, crunchy lift.

- Roughly chop the leaves and stir through a curry or pasta sauce just before serving to add a green boost to a weeknight dinner.

- Finely slice and stir into scrambled eggs or an omelette for a tasty breakfast or last-minute dinner.

Hash browns with silverbeet

5 potatoes, cut into 1 cm cubes

3 tablespoons olive oil

1 red onion, finely chopped

6 bacon rashers, finely chopped

10 silverbeet leaves, stalks finely chopped and leaves roughly shredded

salt and freshly ground black pepper

½ lemon

Preparation time: 15 minutes
Cooking time: 20 minutes
Serves 6

Kids adore hash browns – and parents love kids eating their greens! If you like, substitute the silverbeet with a colourful chard variety or spinach. Pick big leaves of silverbeet, not the baby leaves, as they are better for draping over the hash browns. To speed up this recipe you can cook the potatoes the night before and fry when needed.

Bring a saucepan of water to the boil, add the potatoes and simmer for 5–8 minutes, or until *al dente*. Drain well and pat dry with a tea towel.

Meanwhile, heat 1 tablespoon oil in a heavy-based saucepan over medium heat and sauté the onion, bacon and silverbeet stalks for 3–4 minutes, or until the bacon is cooked and the silverbeet stalks are tender. Add the cooked potatoes and sauté for a further 4–5 minutes, until golden.

Add the shredded silverbeet leaves and remaining oil to a separate frying pan over medium heat. Season with salt and freshly ground black pepper and squeeze over the lemon juice. Cover with a lid and cook for 2 minutes, or until the leaves have wilted.

To serve, pile a mound of the potato mixture into the middle of a plate and drape the wilted silverbeet over the top.

 note

For an even heartier breakfast, place a poached egg on the hash browns, then top with the silverbeet.

Creamy scrambled eggs

8 free-range eggs

½ cup pouring cream

salt and freshly ground black pepper

1 handful chopped mixed herbs,
    such as flat-leaf parsley, chives,
    thyme or chervil

1 tablespoon butter

4 thick slices crusty bread

olive oil

Preparation time: 15 minutes
Cooking time: 10 minutes
Serves 4

Scrambled eggs are an easy and delicious way to feed a crowd on the weekend. With the addition of cream they also make an indulgent breakfast – who doesn't deserve a treat every now and then? Start whisking the eggs and let the kids finish it off – they'll love getting involved and the extra whisking makes for really fluffy eggs.

Whisk the eggs and cream in a bowl and season with salt and freshly ground black pepper. Add the herbs and gently stir to combine.

Melt the butter in a deep non-stick frying pan over low heat until melted and sizzling. Pour the egg mixture into the pan and cook for 2–3 minutes, stirring gently with a wooden spoon. Pull the mixture from the edges back into the middle of the pan – the edges cook faster and you are aiming for even cooking. Stir the eggs enough to scramble but not so much that they resemble breadcrumbs. Remove the pan from the heat just before the eggs are fully set.

Brush both sides of the bread slices with olive oil using a pastry brush and cook on a hot char-grill pan for 2–3 minutes. If you don't have a char-grill pan, toast the bread on a barbecue grill plate, under the grill or in a frying pan.

Serve the scrambled eggs piled on top of the toast with a herb sprig to garnish.

 note

To make this dish a little more decadent, serve with smoked trout or salmon and a dollop of crème fraîche mixed with chives.

Extra special BLT

4 bacon rashers, rind removed
4 free-range eggs
2 tablespoons olive oil
8 slices brown bread
1 avocado, sliced
butter
iceberg lettuce or rocket
2 tomatoes, sliced
freshly ground black pepper

Preparation time: 15 minutes
Cooking time: 10 minutes
Serves 4

This sandwich also makes a great lunch. To jazz it up, use Turkish or sourdough bread. Or to make it easier for little hands, use small rounds of a baguette.

Heat a frying pan or char-grill pan over medium–high heat and fry the bacon for 3–4 minutes, turning occasionally, until just crispy. If you prefer, arrange the bacon on paper towel and cook in the microwave for 60 seconds on high before turning over and cooking for a further 60 seconds.

Heat the olive oil in a clean frying pan over medium heat and crack the eggs into the pan. Fry the eggs for 3–4 minutes, or until the white is set. For a firm yolk, flip the egg and cook for a further 2 minutes.

Spread four slices of bread with avocado and the other four slices with butter. Arrange a bacon rasher on the avocado, then top with an egg, lettuce or rocket and tomato. Season with pepper and top with a buttered slice of bread. Repeat with the remaining ingredients.

Moroccan breakfast couscous

1 cup couscous

1 cup boiling water or hot juice of your choice

½ cup chopped fruit – use a selection of dried apricots, prunes, dates and sultanas

1 teaspoon butter

¼ teaspoon ground cinnamon

1 cup thick plain yoghurt

Preparation time: 10 minutes
Cooking time: 5 minutes
Serves 4

Couscous is a wonderfully versatile ingredient that can be used for both savoury and sweet dishes. This recipe is simple to prepare and super fast. It also makes an impressive brunch dish if you have friends over, and if you need to feed many hungry mouths, simply double or triple the ingredients.

Serve this with some Easy Baked Rhubarb (page 177), a dollop of mascarpone cheese, toasted flaked almonds, preserved peaches, cherries or plums.

Put the couscous in a heatproof bowl and pour over the boiling water or juice, cover with plastic wrap and let it rest for about 5 minutes. Uncover and fluff the couscous with a fork, stirring through the chopped fruit, butter and cinnamon.

Serve the couscous in bowls with a generous dollop of yoghurt on top or on the side. If you are using preserved fruit, drizzle some of the juice over the couscous.

Quick baked beans

3 tablespoons olive oil

½ onion, finely chopped

1 garlic clove, finely chopped

2 teaspoons ground turmeric

3 teaspoons ground cumin

3 teaspoons ground coriander

½ teaspoon allspice

½ teaspoon freshly grated nutmeg

2 teaspoons dried mint

2 bay leaves

440 g can cannellini beans, drained
  and rinsed

440 g can chopped tomatoes

2 teaspoons soft brown sugar

1 cup water

salt and freshly ground black
  pepper

Preparation time: 10 minutes
Cooking time: 25 minutes
Serves 6

If you have a can of cannellini beans to hand, you'll never need to reach for a commercial can of baked beans again. Once you try this homemade version you'll be hooked.

Heat the oil in a saucepan over low–medium heat, add the onion and garlic and fry for 2 minutes. Add the spices, dried mint and bay leaves to the pan and cook for a further 2 minutes, or until aromatic. Add the cannellini beans, tomatoes, sugar and 1 cup water, and season with salt and freshly ground black pepper.

Bring to a simmer then reduce the heat to low, loosely cover with a lid and cook for 20 minutes, stirring occasionally, until thickened. If the mixture is too dry, you may need to add a little extra water. Adjust the seasoning if necessary and serve with toast.

 note

To add a little heat and Latin flavour to this dish, add some freshly chopped chilli or dried chilli flakes to the pan while frying the onion and garlic. Then add some chopped coriander and a squeeze of lime to the mixture just before serving.

Banana and cinnamon porridge

2 cups rolled oats
1 cup milk
1 cinnamon stick
1½ cups water
⅓ cup plain yoghurt
soft brown sugar
1 banana, sliced

Preparation time: 5 minutes
Cooking time: 5 minutes
Serves 4

Porridge makes a terrifically hearty breakfast for kids – helping to keep them energised during the school day. If you like, instead of using the brown sugar to sweeten the porridge, stir through some homemade Strawberry Jam (page 187). For an extra special treat on the weekend, top the porridge with a drizzle of cream, stewed apple or rhubarb and a sprinkle of brown sugar.

Heat the oats, milk and cinnamon in a saucepan with 1½ cups water over medium heat. Bring to the boil, reduce the heat to low and cook for 5–6 minutes, stirring occasionally, until creamy. If the porridge is too thick add an extra 2–3 tablespoons water and stir through.

To serve, spoon the porridge into bowls, add a dollop of yoghurt, sprinkle with brown sugar and top with banana slices.

Sweet lemon pikelets

1 cup plain flour
1 teaspoon baking powder
1 tablespoon caster sugar, plus extra to sprinkle
pinch of salt
zest of ½ lemon
1 egg, lightly whisked
1¼ cups milk
butter
1 lemon, cut into wedges

Preparation time: 15 minutes
Cooking time: 15 minutes
Makes 10 pikelets

We know what you're thinking – this looks like a lot of messing about! But once you've made a few batches of pikelets, this recipe is sure to become a staple. The mixture will keep in the fridge for up to 4 days. Why not double-up and make a batch for the lunchbox at the same time?

Combine the flour, baking powder, sugar, salt and lemon zest in a large bowl. Make a well in the centre and add the egg and milk. Using a whisk, gradually mix the ingredients until smooth and free of lumps. Cover the bowl with plastic wrap and leave in the refrigerator for 30 minutes.

Heat a heavy-based frying pan over medium heat and add 1 teaspoon butter for each pikelet. When the butter is melted and sizzling, add ¼ cup of the mixture for each pikelet to the pan. Let the mixture form its own shape – it should be a circle about the size of your fist. Cook for 2–3 minutes, until the edges start to curl and bubbles appear on the surface. Flip over and cook for a further 2–3 minutes, until golden. Repeat with the remaining batter.

Serve the pikelets warm with a squeeze of lemon juice and a sprinkle of caster sugar.

Kids' lunchboxes

The key to a good lunchbox is planning ahead. It's important to give your kids healthy food to keep their concentration and energy levels up during the day. Opening a lunchbox should make your children happy – keep the variety up and make sure you include some treats now and then. That way, you can guarantee the food will be eaten rather than tossed in the bin.

We often make our sandwiches for the week ahead on a Sunday evening and freeze them – we've listed our top speedy sandwich ideas (see page 28), but there are so many options available.

You can also bake and freeze the muffins, sausage rolls and mini quiches in this section, while the biscuits and slices will keep for a week in an airtight container. You can also make a big batch of Spicy Popcorn on a Sunday for lunchbox and after school snacks during the week.

For something a little different, pack the Mini Ploughman's Lunch for a picnic or school lunch. Traditionally, a ploughman's lunch consists of crusty bread, cheese and pickles, but we've added a few of our own touches. Kids love an interactive way to eat, with lots of different flavours and textures to explore.

Some other, non-traditional fillers for the lunchbox include cherry tomatoes, pickled onions and dill pickles, cream cheese and dips, carrots and celery sticks. Also, break up the monotony of a bread sandwich by using crispbread, wholegrain crackers, tortillas and wraps or a crusty bread roll instead.

Mini ploughman's lunch with country-style pâté

COUNTRY-STYLE PÂTÉ

300 g oyster blade steak, fat trimmed, roughly chopped

salt and freshly ground black pepper

2 tablespoons olive oil

1 onion, finely chopped

2 garlic cloves, finely chopped

1 carrot, grated

2–3 tablespoons tomato sauce

2 tablespoons Worcestershire sauce

PLOUGHMAN'S LUNCH

Pickled Onions (page 197)

dill pickles, Bread and Butter Cucumbers (page 202) or cornichons

assorted cheeses

vegetable sticks, such as carrot, celery, cucumber, capsicum and spring onion

crusty bread

Preparation time: 15 minutes
Cooking time: 20 minutes
Serves 6

We love ploughman's lunches because they provide a healthy, easy and varied meal for our kids – they even make a great dinner alternative on those summer nights that won't cool down. To prepare this for the lunchbox, sandwich biscuits or bread together with the pâté and add a little container of pickles, cheese and vegetable sticks.

Season the steak with salt and freshly ground black pepper. Heat the oil in a saucepan over medium heat and cook the onion and garlic for 2–3 minutes, or until the onion softens. Add the carrot to the pan and sauté for 2–3 minutes. Add the steak, cover, reduce the heat to low and cook for 10–15 minutes, stirring occasionally, until cooked through. Remove from the heat and allow to cool.

Transfer the steak mixture to a food processor, add the tomato and Worcestershire sauces and blend until completely smooth. If the mixture is too dry, add a little more tomato sauce to the mixture. Adjust for seasoning if necessary. The country-style pâté can be stored in an airtight container in the refrigerator for up to 1 week.

Serve the pâté with the other lunch ingredients. The pâté would also make a terrific spread for crusty, grilled bread or served with crackers.

Cheesy tortilla roll-ups

2 tablespoons light cream cheese

1 cup snipped chives or finely
    chopped flat-leaf parsley

1 celery stalk, finely chopped

1 carrot, grated

salt and freshly ground black pepper

6 flour tortillas

250 g shaved ham

2 tomatoes, sliced

Preparation time: 10 minutes
Cooking time: none
Makes 6

Have a batch of this cream cheese mixture in the fridge and whip up these wraps in a couple of minutes as an alternative to a sandwich. Get creative and add mushroom, avocado, alfalfa sprouts, roast chicken, cheese, sultanas, capsicum, cucumber, lettuce – the list is endless.

You can also serve these roll-ups as an after-school snack or an easy dinner. In the warmer months, set everything on platters outside and let the kids construct their own rolls. It may sound like a big mess waiting to happen – but the more often they do it, the better they'll get at it, and kids love to get involved.

Mix the cream cheese in a bowl with the chives or parsley. Add the celery and carrot, season with salt and freshly ground black pepper and combine well.

Spread the tortillas with the cream cheese mixture, top with the shaved ham and tomato, roll up and serve.

LETTUCE AND ROCKET

It can be tricky to get kids to eat their greens, but in the case of lettuce and rocket you'll have far more of a chance if the kids have helped you plant, water and pick them. Lettuce and rocket should be the staples of every vegetable patch or pot – they grow year-round, have a delicious, fresh flavour and make a beautiful decorative border or under-planting in pots.

Soil and site

It's crucial that lettuce and rocket are protected from strong sun and winds. Lettuce and rocket need nitrogen so feed the soil well with compost, blood and bone or poultry manure six weeks before planting. Adding organic matter when the seedlings are growing will burn the baby plants. If you have prepared the soil well, you shouldn't need to fertilise regularly, but you may want to give the plants a top-up with a complete fertiliser or a seaweed solution coming up to the height of summer, so they stay strong and healthy. Some people recommend fertilising fortnightly, but this is only necessary if you have poor soil.

Planting

The optimum growing temperature for lettuce and rocket is around 20°C, with spring, early summer and autumn the best times for planting. Avoid planting seeds or seedlings in the extremes of winter or summer.

If you want to have a constant supply of salad greens throughout spring, summer and autumn, stagger your planting every fortnight – a punnet or two of six to eight plants each time should see a family covered during the warmer months.

Lettuce and rocket both look lovely grown in pots or half wine barrels. Lettuces are also great plants for small areas and can keep you going all summer with just a couple of pots and regular planting. Use premium standard potting mix, mulch well, add water-saving crystals and water regularly so the pots don't dry out.

Growing

Companion plant lettuce and rocket with carrot, onion, strawberry and beetroot. It's also advisable to plant lettuce under taller crops, such as tomatoes, corn and brussels sprouts, so they don't get scorched by the summer sun.

Salad greens need to be well tended, as the leaves will be bitter and quickly go to seed if they have to struggle for moisture and nutrients. Water is vital, so get the kids to regularly water the salad leaves using small buckets or watering cans.

Pests

Watch out for slugs and snails as they love the tender little leaves of these salad greens. Try scattering the ground around the plants with coffee grinds or broken eggshells – snails and slugs hate crawling over gritty and dry textures. You can also leave small tubs or saucers with beer around the plants as snails are attracted to the amber nectar and drown. If all else fails, you can kill them with a non-toxic Chilli Spray (page 72) or Garlic Spray (page 107).

Aphids can also be a troublesome pest for rocket and lettuce. The easiest solution for ridding the garden of these common nasties is by planting orange nasturtiums and marigolds as their scent drives the insects away. Nasturtiums are also easy to grow and look lovely as a border, or spilling over pots on a balcony.

Harvesting

It's best to harvest tender plants such as rocket and lettuce in the morning as the leaves may be wilted and inedible if harvested in the heat of the midday sun. Lettuce and rocket will be ready to harvest within two months of planting seeds and within one month of planting seedlings. You can harvest the outer leaves, but we generally pick the whole plant.

Harvest rocket regularly – the more you pick the more it will grow. You can cut leaves off the plant, or cut down to about 15 cm and wait for new leaves to shoot. Rocket leaves are tastiest when they are young. Look out for the wild varieties of rocket, often labelled 'arugula'.

Allow rocket to develop their lovely white flowers and go to seed. It makes the garden look pretty, if a little wild and wooly. Get the kids to help you collect and crush the seed pods and replant them in the garden.

Or if you want to go for the easier option, you can just let the rocket go to seed and wait for the new plants to pop up in your garden bed or pot. Letting rocket perpetually move through this cycle will mean you have a permanent supply. We let rocket just naturally move through the growing cycle – it fills up the gaps in our garden beds and it means we always have a supply.

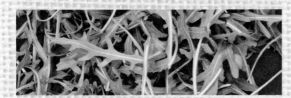

Quick ways with lettuce and rocket

- Raw baby rocket leaves add a delicious peppery flavour to salads.
- Chop rocket leaves and stir through a pasta sauce just before serving to add some greens to a lazy dinner.
- Wrap cooked prawns with herbs in crispy lettuce leaves and serve with an Asian dipping sauce.
- Substitute rocket for basil for a tasty pesto.
- Arrange iceberg lettuce wedges on a plate and drizzle with a creamy blue cheese dressing – 1 cup sour cream, 50 g blue cheese, juice of 1 lemon, salt and freshly ground black pepper to taste.

Crunchy chicken and cheese lettuce cups

1 barbecued chicken, meat shredded
¾ cup grated cheddar cheese
1 carrot, grated
salt and freshly ground black pepper
1 iceberg lettuce

Preparation time: 10 minutes
Cooking time: none
Serves 6

These lettuce cups make an excellent alternative to the traditional chicken sandwich in the lunchbox – and kids adore the crunch factor. Pack them in a container so they don't get squashed in the school bag.

Combine the shredded chicken in a large bowl with the cheese and carrot, then season with salt and freshly ground black pepper.

Carefully pull the iceberg lettuce apart, allowing 1 or 2 lettuce cups per person. Immerse the lettuce in iced water for 20 minutes, until crispy. Remove and pat dry with a tea towel.

Spoon the chicken mixture into the lettuce cups and serve. Alternatively, get the kids to assemble them.

 notes

To give this an Asian twist, leave out the cheese and add some cooked vermicelli noodles, roasted and chopped peanuts and fresh herbs such as coriander or mint to the chicken.

To make a quick and tasty dipping sauce for the rolls, combine 2 teaspoons sesame oil, 1 tablespoon fish sauce, juice of 1 lime, ½ teaspoon soft brown sugar and 1 tablespoon sweet chilli sauce.

Mini cheese and bacon quiches

3 tablespoons olive oil, plus extra
    to grease the moulds

½ onion, finely chopped

1 garlic clove, finely chopped

4 bacon rashers, finely chopped

1 small zucchini, finely chopped

2–3 silverbeet or chard leaves
    (or 2 handfuls baby spinach),
    finely chopped

3 flat-leaf parsley sprigs, stalks
    discarded, leaves finely chopped

8 eggs

½ cup pouring cream

salt and freshly ground black pepper

6 sheets frozen puff pastry,
    defrosted

2 cups grated cheddar cheese

Preparation time: 15 minutes
Cooking time: 30 minutes
Makes 12

These quiches make a great addition to the lunchbox, they taste terrific and can be made on the weekend when you've got more time. Serve them cold in summer with cherry tomatoes and cucumber cubes. In winter, heat the quiches up before school in the microwave or oven, then pack them into an insulated lunchbox so they stay warm until lunch time.

Preheat the oven to 180°C. Heat the oil in a frying pan over medium heat and cook the onion, garlic and bacon for 2–3 minutes, or until the onion softens. Add the zucchini, silverbeet and parsley to the pan and cook for 3–4 minutes, or until the silverbeet wilts. Remove from the heat and allow to cool slightly.

Meanwhile, whisk the eggs and cream in a bowl and season with salt and freshly ground black pepper. Pour the egg mixture into the cooled vegetable mixture and combine well.

Grease all the holes in a standard 12-hole muffin tin. Cut out 12 rounds from the pastry using a saucer with a diameter of 13 cm. This will give you an overhang of about 3 cm over the side of the muffin tin. Pinch together and squeeze this overhang around the edge of the muffin circle to create a lip. Using a ladle, evenly spoon the mixture between each pastry case, until about two-thirds full. Sprinkle the grated cheese over the top.

Bake for 25 minutes, or until golden and cooked through. To test, insert a skewer into the middle of a quiche – it should come out clean. Remove from the oven and cool in the tin for 10 minutes before transferring to a wire rack to cool completely.

These quiches will store in an airtight container in the refrigerator for 3–4 days, or can be frozen for up to 3 months. Reheat in a 160°C oven for 10 minutes, or simply serve cold.

 notes

This mixture also makes at least 40 mini quiches if you use a mini muffin tin.

Chinese chicken salad

1½ × 85 g packets instant noodles
1 carrot, grated
¼ cucumber, finely sliced
12 snow peas, cut into long strips
2 cups shredded cooked chicken

SAUCE
1 teaspoon sesame oil
2 tablespoons soy sauce
1 tablespoon sweet chilli sauce
juice of 1 lemon or lime
½ teaspoon soft brown sugar

Preparation time: 15 minutes
Cooking time: none
Makes about 4 cups

This salad is quick to prepare, keeps in the fridge for days and is perfect for a sandwich substitute in the lunchbox. Experiment with the vegetables in this salad – it's an excellent way to try out new flavours and textures. Ask your kids to help you choose from your vegie garden or the greengrocer, as being involved often helps fussy eaters overcome their concerns.

Roughly crush the noodles in the packet and combine in a bowl with the carrot, cucumber, snow peas and chicken.

In a small bowl, whisk the sauce ingredients together and pour over the noodle salad. Add 2–3 tablespoons water to the empty sauce bowl and swish around to catch the remaining ingredients. Pour over the salad and stir through until all the ingredients are well coated.

Cover with plastic wrap and store in the refrigerator overnight. Before putting into containers for the lunchbox, give the salad a quick stir to redistribute the sauce.

* notes

Feel free to vary the vegetable component of this salad – try thinly sliced red and green capsicum, bean shoots, thinly sliced celery, blanched and thinly sliced green beans or baby spinach leaves.

The great thing about this salad is its adaptability to your family's tastes. To give it a little more Asian flair for the adults, add chopped coriander, mint, spring onion and some finely sliced red chilli.

Corn and cumin muffins

2 corn cobs (or 1 cup corn kernels)

1½ cups grated cheddar cheese

2 flat-leaf parsley sprigs, leaves finely chopped and stalks discarded

2 teaspoons ground cumin

½ teaspoon each salt and freshly ground black pepper

2 cups self-raising flour

½ teaspoon baking powder

1 cup milk

1 egg

½ cup olive oil

Preparation time: 15 minutes
Cooking time: 10 minutes
Makes 12 large or 36 mini muffins

These delicious savoury muffins are great to make with the kids on the weekend – and give you plenty of lunchbox options for the week.

Preheat the oven to 180°C. Line a standard 12-hole muffin tin with paper cases. Slice the corn off the cob and combine in a bowl with the cheese, parsley, cumin, salt and freshly ground black pepper.

Put the flour and baking powder into a bowl and make a well in the centre. Add the milk, egg and oil to the flour and combine well before adding the corn mixture. Stir until combined.

Divide the mixture evenly between the paper cases and tap the tray on the bench to even out the mixture. Bake for 10–12 minutes, or until a skewer comes out clean. These muffins will store in an airtight container in the refrigerator or pantry for up to 5 days.

 note

Make some garlic butter for the muffins by combining 2 tablespoons softened butter, 1 crushed garlic clove, a pinch of salt and 1 teaspoon finely chopped flat-leaf parsley.

Sweet apple and cinnamon muffins

1½ cups finely chopped apple

2 teaspoons ground cinnamon or nutmeg

½ cup caster sugar

2 cups self-raising flour

½ teaspoon salt

½ teaspoon baking powder

¾ cup milk

1 egg

½ cup olive oil

Preparation time: 15 minutes
Cooking time: 15 minutes
Makes 12 large or 36 mini muffins

These muffins are a great choice for a lunchbox treat. If you like, make mini muffins instead, which will only take 5–6 minutes to cook.

Preheat the oven to 180°C. Line a standard 12-hole muffin tin with paper cases. Combine the apple in a bowl with the cinnamon and sugar.

Put the flour, salt and baking powder into a bowl and make a well in the centre. Add the milk, egg and oil to the flour mixture and combine well before adding the apple mixture. Stir until combined.

Divide the mixture evenly between the paper cases and tap the tray on the bench to even out the mixture. Bake for 12–15 minutes, or until a skewer comes out clean. These muffins will store in an airtight container in the pantry for up to 5 days.

 note

Make some cinnamon butter for the muffins by combining 1 tablespoon softened butter, 1 tablespoon caster sugar and 1 teaspoon ground cinnamon.

Speedy Sandwich Ideas

Shaved ham, spinach and Swiss cheese

Vegemite and alfalfa sprouts on buttered brown bread.

Grated carrot and cheddar cheese

Cream cheese, shredded lettuce and finely sliced celery

Quick chicken salad

Peanut butter, honey and butter

Cold cuts with chutney and lettuce

Mashed hard-boiled eggs combined with mayonnaise, celery, capsicum, spring onion and shredded spinach

Chicken bacon and avocado

Finely sliced corned beef and cucumber

Chocoholic cranberry Anzacs

125 g butter

1 tablespoon golden syrup

2 tablespoons boiling water

1 cup wholemeal self-raising flour

1 cup soft brown sugar

1 cup rolled oats

1 cup dried cranberries, roughly chopped

1 cup shredded coconut

¾ cup good-quality dark chocolate buds

pinch of salt

1 tablespoon wheatgerm (optional)

1 teaspoon bicarbonate of soda

Preparation time: 15 minutes
Cooking time: 15 minutes
Makes about 30

These biscuits are delicious, healthy and quick, so for lunchboxes or snacks they tick all the right boxes. This is also a great recipe for the kids to try on their own as they'll need limited supervision and will be so pleased with the results.

Preheat the oven to 160°C. Lightly grease or line 2 baking trays with baking paper. Heat the butter and golden syrup in a saucepan over low heat for 2–3 minutes, or until the butter melts. Add the boiling water, stir to combine and remove from the heat.

Combine all the dry ingredients in a large bowl and make a well in the centre. Pour the melted butter mixture into the dry ingredients and mix thoroughly to a firm consistency. Using a spoon and clean hands, roll and squeeze the mixture into about 30 walnut-sized balls and arrange on the prepared trays, leaving space between the biscuits to spread.

Cook for 8–10 minutes, or until golden brown, swapping the arrangement of the trays halfway through to allow for even cooking. Remove from the oven and cool on the trays for 10 minutes to harden the biscuits. Transfer to a wire rack, without stacking, to cool completely. These biscuits will store in an airtight container for up to 7 days. The uncooked mixture will store in the freezer for up to 4 weeks.

Spicy popcorn

50 g butter

1 tablespoon olive oil

2 tablespoons mild curry powder

1 teaspoon salt

1 teaspoon ground cumin

12 cups popped popcorn (about 1 cup raw kernels)

100 g fried noodles (see Note)

Preparation time: 10 minutes
Cooking time: 15 minutes
Makes 12 cups

This is a tasty and easy snack that stores well in the lunchbox. It keeps for 2–3 days in an airtight container and also makes a great nibble food for a kid's party.

Preheat the oven to 60°C. Melt the butter and oil in a saucepan over medium heat, add the curry powder, salt and cumin and stir for 2–3 minutes, or until aromatic. Combine the popcorn and noodles in a bowl then pour in the spice and butter mixture. Mix well, then arrange the popcorn in one layer on a baking tray. Heat in the oven for 10–15 minutes, until it has dried out a little and has some crunch.

 note

Ready fried noodles can be found in the Asian section of most large supermarkets.

Chewy muesli and apricot slice

185 g butter
2 tablespoons golden syrup
½ cup untoasted muesli
½ cup self-raising flour
¼ cup rolled oats
¼ cup desiccated coconut
125 g dried apricots, finely chopped
½ cup soft brown sugar
2 eggs, lightly beaten

Preparation time: 10 minutes
Cooking time: 40 minutes
Makes 30 squares

Kirsty's mother-in-law Sue used to make this for her two boys. Now she makes it for her grandchildren for morning or afternoon tea. Two generations can't be wrong. This slice is great for younger children to make with adult supervision – it helps to hone skills in measuring ingredients and mixing.

Preheat the oven to 180°C. Grease a 16 × 26 cm slice tin. Melt the butter and golden syrup in a saucepan over low heat for 2–3 minutes.

Combine the muesli, flour, oats, coconut, apricots and sugar in a large bowl. Pour the butter mixture into the muesli mixture and combine, then stir through the beaten eggs. Spread the mixture evenly over the base of the prepared tin.

Bake for 40 minutes, or until the slice shrinks slightly from the sides of the tin. Cool in the tin then cut into 3 cm squares. Store in an airtight container for up to 1 week.

Energy slice

150 g butter
1 tablespoon honey
1 cup rolled oats
1 cup sultanas
½ cup wholemeal self-raising flour
½ cup raw or soft brown sugar
½ cup desiccated coconut

Preparation time: 10 minutes
Cooking time: 30 minutes
Makes 30 squares

Keep an airtight container of this energy slice on hand to add to the lunchbox or for an after-school treat. But this slice is not just for kids – try a piece with a cup of tea or coffee and you'll be hooked too! It's an energy hit for the whole family.

Preheat the oven to 180°C. Grease a 16 × 26 cm slice tin. Melt the butter and honey in a saucepan over low heat for 2–3 minutes.

Combine the remaining ingredients in a large bowl. Pour the butter and honey mixture into the oat mixture and mix well. Spread evenly over the base of the prepared tin.

Bake for 30 minutes, or until the surface is evenly brown. Cool in the tin then cut into 3 cm squares. Keep slices in an airtight container for up to 1 week or freeze in individual portions for up to 1 month.

Easy sausage rolls

250 g beef mince

1 onion, roughly chopped

2 garlic cloves, roughly chopped

1 carrot, grated

1 zucchini, grated

3 silverbeet or chard leaves
   (or 2 handfuls baby spinach),
   finely chopped

1 cup roughly chopped flat-leaf
   parsley

½ cup dry breadcrumbs
   (or 2 tablespoons plain flour)

⅓ cup tomato sauce

2 eggs

salt and freshly ground black pepper

2 sheets frozen puff pastry,
   defrosted

Preparation time: 20 minutes
Cooking time: 30 minutes
Makes 4 large rolls

These versatile pastries can be a lunchbox treat, an after-school snack or party fare. They also offer a great opportunity to 'value add' in the vegetable department! If you want to keep the sausage rolls warm until lunch time, heat them in the microwave for 1 minute, then pack them into an insulated lunchbox.

Preheat the oven to 200°C. Lightly grease or line a baking tray with baking paper. Place the mince, onion and garlic in a food processor and pulse until well combined. Add the carrot, zucchini, silverbeet, parsley, breadcrumbs, tomato sauce, one of the eggs and salt and freshly ground black pepper. Process until smooth.

Make an egg wash by mixing the remaining egg with 1 tablespoon water in a bowl. Cut each sheet of pastry in half to make 4 even pieces. Leave a 2.5 cm strip of pastry around all the edges. Spoon the mixture lengthwise along the pastry. Form it into an even mound, like a sausage. Fold the edge closest to you over the mixture lengthwise and roll up until the edges meet. Brush the end with the egg wash and press firmly together. Repeat with the remaining pastry and mixture.

Brush the tops of the sausage rolls with the egg wash and arrange on the prepared baking tray. Pierce a few holes into the tops of the rolls with a skewer. Bake for 20–30 minutes, or until golden and flaky. Allow to cool slightly before serving. If desired, cut the rolls in half for individual lunches, or into bite-sized pieces for a party.

✳ notes

If you prefer, pork, lamb or chicken mince can be substituted for the beef. Include herbs such as marjoram, rosemary, thyme or whatever you have growing in the garden. Otherwise, you may want to add feta cheese to the mixture or some chopped chilli to make a spicier sausage roll.

For a Indian-style vegetarian version, substitute the meat component for finely diced potato, parsnip and swede, and add 2 teaspoons Indian-style curry powder.

Soups

We think of soup as love in a bowl!
It's so satisfying to see your kids tucking into
a bowl of warm, nutritious soup.

This section is full of soups that burst with
flavour, but are not too taxing on your time or
budget. Double the recipes and freeze half for
those nights when you need something super-
fast. Most soups taste better the next day, so any
leftovers will be a great treat. All of these soups
freeze well and should keep in the freezer for at
least two months.

With many soups you can use whatever vegetable
is in season. We've included a Quick Roasted
Tomato Soup for when you have a glut of
tomatoes in your garden at the end of summer.
Or for the colder months there's luscious Cream
of Cauliflower Soup. Of course, no soup section
is complete without 'mothers' cure' in a bowl:
chicken soup. We have two variations: Asian-style
Chicken and Sweetcorn Broth and Mediterranean
Chicken Soup – because we can't get enough
of the good stuff!

Warming pea and ham soup

3 tablespoons olive oil

1 large leek, white part only, finely
    chopped

2 garlic cloves, finely chopped

6 streaky bacon rashers, finely
    chopped

2 carrots, finely chopped

4 celery stalks, finely chopped

1 ½ cups split green peas

1 large smoked ham hock
    (about 700 g), cut in half (ask
    your butcher)

2 bay leaves

salt and freshly ground black pepper

Preparation time: 20 minutes
Cooking time: 2–2½ hours
Serves 6

As the days get shorter and cooler, we head inside to make this family favourite. Make a pot and keep it going for a couple of days for weekend lunches or a quick dinner after footy or netball practice. Offer the kids a little cup to warm their tummies after a few hours playing outside in the cold.

Heat the oil in a large, heavy-based saucepan over medium heat and sauté the leek, garlic, bacon, carrot and celery for 5–6 minutes, or until the vegetables have softened.

Add the split peas and ham hock to the pan and pour in 3 litres water. Add the bay leaves and season with salt and freshly ground black pepper. Increase the heat to high, bring to the boil then immediately reduce the heat to low. Cover partially with a lid and simmer for 2 hours, skimming off any impurities with a large spoon, until the soup is thick and the meat is falling off the bone.

If the soup is too thick for your liking, add ½ cup water at a time until it reaches your preferred consistency. If you do add extra water, simmer for at least another 20 minutes on low and taste for seasoning. This is also handy for reheating, as pea and ham soup can thicken once it cools down.

Remove the bone and, using tongs or a fork, pull as much meat off the bone as possible. Return the meat to the soup, discarding the bone. Reheat the soup and taste for seasoning – ham hocks can be salty so be cautious when adding salt. Serve with hot crusty bread for dipping, or allow to cool and store in the freezer for up to 2 months.

Asian-style chicken and sweetcorn broth

1 kg whole chicken

3 tablespoons olive oil

4 garlic cloves, finely chopped

1 large onion, finely diced

2 cm knob of ginger, finely chopped

2 large carrots, finely diced

2 celery stalks, finely diced

200 g chicken necks (ask your butcher)

5 whole coriander sprigs with roots, leaves removed

1/3 cup light soy sauce

440 g can corn kernels, drained (or kernels from 4 corn cobs)

freshly ground black pepper

sesame oil

1 handful chopped coriander leaves

2 spring onions, thinly sliced

Preparation time: 30 minutes
Cooking time: 2 hours
Serves 6–8

This soup is truly restorative – you can feel it helping your body with every mouthful – while the ginger, coriander, soy and sesame impart a lovely Asian flavour. To make this soup in half the time, use 10 large, skinless drumsticks instead of a whole chicken. We realise the chicken necks might be a little off-putting, but they add an incredible depth of flavour.

Remove and discard the skin and tail from the chicken. Remove the neck and set aside. Rinse the chicken well.

Heat the oil in a large saucepan over medium heat and sauté the garlic, onion, ginger, carrot and celery for 8–10 minutes, or until the vegetables soften.

Add the chicken, chicken necks and coriander sprigs to the pan with enough cold water to just cover the ingredients (about 3 litres). Increase the heat to high, bring to the boil then immediately reduce the heat to low. Cover partially with a lid and simmer for 1½ hours, skimming off any impurities with a spoon, until the chicken is falling off the bone.

Remove and discard the chicken necks and coriander sprigs from the pan. Remove the whole chicken and, using tongs or a fork, pull as much meat off the carcass as possible. Return the meat to the soup, discarding the carcass.

Add the soy sauce and corn to the pan. Bring the soup back to a simmer for 15 minutes, skimming off any impurities with a spoon – the soup should start to look clear. Taste for seasoning and add some freshly ground black pepper to taste. You won't need to add salt as the soy sauce is salty enough.

Ladle the soup into bowls and stir through a few more drops of soy sauce and 1 drop of sesame oil. Top with chopped coriander and spring onion and serve immediately.

 note

To create a heartier meal for a casual dinner or lunch add 80–100 g crushed dried noodles to the pan when returning the meat to the soup.

TOMATOES

Tomatoes are the stars of the garden during summer. Kids love to pick and eat the cute cherry varieties straight off the vine – so you'll need at least four plants if you want any tomatoes to make it to the dinner table.

Tomatoes are relatively easy to grow and harvest, and they taste so delicious that you won't be choosing commercially-grown varieties again. Home gardeners are creating a demand for the old-fashioned heirloom varieties of tomato that you rarely see at supermarkets. This means that today you can enjoy yellow, orange, pink, purple, black, green, white and striped tomatoes, as well as standard red varieties.

Bush varieties of tomato can be planted in pots, hanging baskets or any outdoor spot, and they are perfect for the family as you can just let them grow wild. The more traditional tomato varieties grow upwards in a straight line and will need staking to support the plant as it grows.

Tomatoes can be eaten plain, added to salads, grilled or finely chopped to make bruschetta. They go brilliantly with Mediterranean herbs such as chives, basil, thyme and parsley. If you still have unripened tomatoes on the vine when the cool weather hits at the end of the growing season, use them to make the deliciously acidic Green Tomato Pickles (page 198).

Also, if you've been out in the garden for too long and are feeling a little sunburnt, generations of Aussie gardeners swear that fresh tomato rubbed directly onto sunburn takes away the sting and soothes the skin.

Soil and site

Lots of sun, protection from the wind and well-drained soil are the most important factors for successful tomato growing. Make sure you add manure or compost (or both) to your soil about six weeks before planting the tomatoes. Dig the fertiliser in well and let it break down as tomatoes tend to suck the nutrients out of the soil. Boost the soil with an organic source of phosphorus or potash – tomatoes need plenty to thrive.

Many nurseries sell special self-contained grow-bags that sit easily on a balcony or courtyard and are perfect for growing tomatoes. If you're planting seedlings into pots, use premium grade potting mix and mix some manure in six weeks prior to give the soil a boost.

Never plant tomatoes in exactly the same spot or soil year after year. The roots are prone to nematodes – microscopic soil organisms that can stunt root growth. Crop rotation is important for tomatoes, so alternate years with silverbeet or chard, corn, *brassicas* or onions. Never alternate with potatoes as the soil from both potatoes and tomatoes needs a break after each crop.

Planting

Tomato seedlings should either be planted in spring, after all the frosts have finished, or during early summer. Aim to plant seeds at least two months before the last frost for your area (tomatoes hate the cold and their fruit won't set). Or alternatively, at least two months before you plan to plant them outside. Tomato seeds need a minimum of 15°C to germinate.

Plant four seeds in 10–15 cm pots or in a specialist seedling tray. Keep the seedlings moist and protected in a warm, sunny spot such as a sun-drenched windowsill, protected verandah or greenhouse until it is warm enough to plant them into the garden. You may like to cover the pots with plastic wrap until the plants shoot – it's an easy way of replicating a greenhouse environment.

The seedlings will be ready to plant out when the frosts have finished and they are about 10 cm tall. Don't take seedlings you have grown from scratch and plant them straight into the garden – they won't like the rapid change of temperature and conditions. Rather, 'harden off' the plants for a couple days by placing the seedlings outside for a few hours each day to acclimatise before planting out.

Plant the seedlings at least 50 cm apart, or even more for the bushier varieties. Check the instructions with your punnet or seed packet as they vary.

Growing

The secret to perfect tomatoes is keeping the soil consistently moist. 'Little and often' is the key to watering tomatoes, especially when the fruit is ripening, rather than occassionally giving the plants a deep soak. Uneven watering will cause the fruit to warp and split open.

Companion plant tomatoes with parsley, chives, basil and celery to keep the plants strong and vigorous. These plants make great companions at the table too. Tomatoes won't thrive if they're planted near potatoes or rosemary, so it's best to steer clear if you can.

Bush tomato varieties planted in garden beds or special grow bags can be left to their own devices after planting – just make sure you keep the watering consistent. If you have planted them in pots or hanging baskets, you'll need to feed them once or twice in the growing season with a specialist tomato fertiliser or seaweed solution just to keep the plants perky. You can nip some of the offshoots and branches if you want to stop the bush becoming too unwieldy.

Standard vine tomato plants will need support as soon as they are over about 10–15 cm, otherwise they will just blow over in the wind. You can use wooden or bamboo garden stakes, tie the stem to a trellis or even use a drainpipe or balcony railing if you're growing tomatoes in pots. Pull the lower leaves off as the plant grows up, but be sure to keep a strong canopy of leaves so the fruit doesn't get too hot.

Traditional tomato plants will need some initial nurturing with plenty of organic matter in the soil and a dose of potash or seaweed solution at the seedling stage. But don't go overboard with the fertiliser during the growing season. Tomatoes grow well with just the right combination of soil, sun and water, leaving you more time to enjoy the fruit with your family.

Pests

To prevent the occurance or spreading of fungal diseases, always water tomato plants very low to the ground. Tomato plants hate their overhanging leaves (and fruit) being wet.

If the soil is good, and the tomatoes are planted in a protected, sunny climate, tomatoes will pretty much take care of themselves. Fruit fly is a major pest, but you can protect your tomatoes by using a commercial organic spray or dust commonly available at all nurseries. Alternatively, keep the flies away by covering the fruit on the vine with paper bags.

Watch out for slugs – there's nothing worse than your perfect crop being studded with holes (except perhaps biting into a juicy tomato only to have the bitter taste of slug in your mouth). For a non-toxic remedy to rid your plants of these nasties, try a homemade Chilli Spray (page 72) or Garlic Spray (page 107).

The other major pest issue with tomatoes is nematodes, which hamper root growth. You can buy resistant varieties of tomatoes but you can also combat this problem by preparing the soil properly using crop rotation, such as alternate plantings annually with mustard seed, *brassicas* or silverbeet.

Harvesting

Tomatoes should be ripe within three months of the seedling stage. Excessive heat or cold can delay the fruit setting from the flowers, but the growing season is straightforward. Pick when the plants are red (if it's a standard variety), and use the last of the green fruit for pickles (page 198).

Quick ways with tomatoes

- Slice a mixture of red and green tomatoes and arrange on a plate, drizzle with olive oil and sprinkle with a little salt for the perfect side salad. Serve with crusty bread.
- Finely dice and stir through a Thai green curry or pasta sauce just before serving.
- Finely dice and stir into scrambled eggs or an omelette for a healthy breakfast or fast dinner.
- Use leftover green tomatoes at the end of the season to make into pickles and chutney.

Quick roasted tomato soup

2 red onions, roughly chopped

2 whole garlic bulbs, ends sliced off

20 large tomatoes (beef, hollow or
    round varieties), roughly chopped

1 long red chilli, seeds removed
    and chopped

2 teaspoons soft brown sugar

3–4 tablespoons extra virgin olive oil

salt and freshly ground black pepper

3–4 cups good-quality low-salt
    chicken stock

1 handful chopped basil leaves

Preparation time: 15 minutes
Cooking time: 45 minutes
Serves 6–8

This is a wonderful way to use end-of-season tomatoes when you have a glut. This recipe is intentionally large so that you can freeze half – perfect for a quick meal on a cool night. The sauce can also double as a tomato passata – stir through cooked pasta with basil, sausage and lots of grated parmesan. If you want to make this soup out of tomato-growing season, simply replace the fresh tomatoes with two large cans of good-quality tomatoes.

Preheat the oven to 160°C. Combine the onion, garlic, tomato and chilli in an ovenproof baking dish. Sprinkle with the sugar, drizzle with the oil and season with salt and freshly ground black pepper. Cover with foil and bake for 30 minutes. Remove the foil and cook for a further 10 minutes, or until the tomato has begun to caramelise.

Remove from the oven and allow to cool slightly. Squeeze the garlic out of the roasted cloves into the bowl of a food processor, add the other roasted ingredients and purée until completely smooth.

Bring 3 cups stock and the puréed ingredients to a simmer in a saucepan over medium heat. If needed, add more hot stock until you reach your desired consistency. Season with salt and freshly ground black pepper, and stir through the basil just before serving.

✳ **note**

To give this soup a Moroccan feel add ½ cup couscous while it simmers and serve with a squeeze of lemon juice and a large handful of chopped mint leaves.

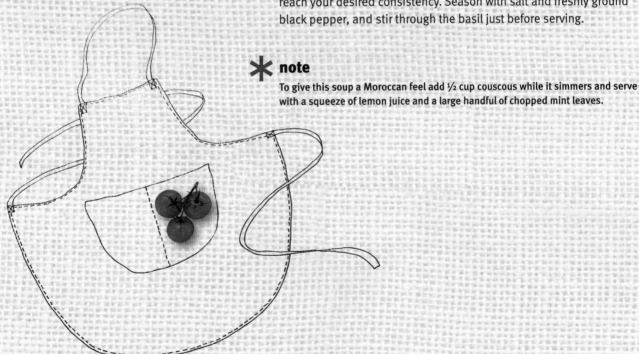

Hearty minestrone

⅓ cup olive oil

1 onion, finely chopped

1 leek, white part only, finely
   chopped

6 bacon rashers, finely chopped

3 garlic cloves, finely chopped

2 celery stalks, finely chopped

1 potato, finely chopped

2 carrots, finely chopped

1 swede, finely chopped

5 silverbeet leaves, stalks finely
   chopped and leaves shredded

2 tablespoons tomato paste

2 bay leaves

2 × 440 g cans chopped tomatoes

1 cup roughly chopped flat-leaf
   parsley

salt and freshly ground black pepper

10 green beans, cut into 1 cm lengths

1 cup crushed spaghetti or
   other pasta

grated parmesan cheese

Preparation time: 30 minutes
Cooking time: 1 hour 10 minutes
Serves 8

You'll need to raid the vegetable patch for this delicious soup, a great all-rounder that helps to boost winter immunity. The bacon imparts a smoky flavour, the pasta fills everyone up and you can any vegetables from your garden or greengrocer according to what's in season.

Heat the oil in a large saucepan over medium heat and sauté the onion, leek, bacon and garlic for 7–8 minutes. Add the celery, potato, carrot and swede to the pan and sauté for a further 4–5 minutes. Add the chopped silverbeet stalks and tomato paste and stir to combine.

Add 2 litres water, the bay leaves, tomatoes and half the parsley to the pan. Season with salt and freshly ground black pepper. Increase the heat to high, bring to the boil, then reduce the heat to low, partially cover with a lid and simmer for 45 minutes.

Add the beans, shredded silverbeet leaves, crushed spaghetti and remaining parsley to the pan and simmer for a further 10 minutes, or until the beans and pasta are cooked.

Adjust the seasoning to taste and serve with parmesan on the side.

 note

To make some cheesy croutons, fry slices of baguette in olive oil until golden and crisp. As soon as they come out of the pan, rub a cut garlic clove over the bread. Top the croutons with a mixture of grated parmesan and cheddar cheeses and pop them under the grill for 2 minutes, or until the cheese is bubbly. To serve, place a cheesy crouton into each bowl.

BROCCOLI +

CAULIFLOWER AND BROCCOLI

When the temperature drops we tend to crave comfort food, such as steaming bowls of soups or curries, slow-bakes and roasts. Fortunately, the two stars of the garden during the cooler months – cauliflower and broccoli – are versatile and hearty vegetables that lend themselves to many styles of cooking. They also give little growing bodies plenty of energy to run around outside on those cold winter days.

Cauliflower and broccoli are cool season crops, planted from late summer to autumn for harvesting right through from autumn to spring. However, if you're a diehard brassica fan, it is possible to grow a crop year round if you hunt out modern varieties.

Today, there are many cauliflower varieties to choose from – standard white, purple, lime green, cream and broccoli crosses. If your kids baulk at the traditional white variety, why not grow a couple of novelty colours and get them to choose the one they want for dinner? Freshly picked and steamed cauliflower needs no other adornment than butter or olive oil, salt and freshly ground black pepper.

Like cauliflower, broccoli is one of the staples for any family vegetable patch. The florets are as ornamental as any flower – a row of broccoli standing tall and proud in your garden looks grand indeed.

There are white, purple and green varieties available, along with the sprouting, or Calabrese, varieties. Chinese broccoli, gai lan and broccolini are also popular varieties that make a tasty and vibrant accompaniment to any Asian-inspired meal.

The beauty of broccoli is that is has a heavy yield – just four plants can supply a family of five with weeknight vegetables for a few weeks. We suggest staggering the planting, so you have at least four plants on the go from autumn to spring.

Soil and site
Cauliflower needs careful tending and feeding to get the floral heads to develop to a decent size. Broccoli, however, doesn't need the same attention.

In both cases, you'll need well-composted and fertilised soil, plenty of drainage and, depending on your soil, you may also need to throw in a complete fertiliser before planting. Water regularly, but make sure the soil isn't boggy as you'll rot the roots of the plant.

Cauliflower and broccoli will struggle in acidic soil, so add a commercial lime solution at least two months before planting. Never add lime and manure at the same time as the chemicals react and produce a noxious gas.

Never stress cauliflower or broccoli with too little water or nutrients in the soil, as the heads will grow warped and bobbly and may even shoot straight to seed.

Planting
Like all brassicas, broccoli and cauliflower thrive in cool climates or temperate areas – they won't cope in extreme heat, so don't plant seeds or seedlings until the peak of summer has passed.

We recommend planting in autumn, for harvesting right through winter and early spring. It's possible to plant broccoli year-round using different varieties, but we haven't had the same success growing broccoli over summer. The florets tend to be tiny and irregular.

Seeds sown in punnets will germinate in about a fortnight. Plant three to four seeds in 10 cm pots from the outset and wait for the seedlings to grow to 10 cm before planting out in the garden. As always, leave the pots in the garden for a couple of hours each day to allow the seedlings to acclimatise before planting into the beds. Make sure the plants are fully established in the garden before the heavy winter frosts set in.

It's easiest to grow cauliflower and broccoli from seedlings purchased from the nursery. Just check that all the leaves look strong and are not wilted or yellowing. Plant directly into the garden bed, and give a liquid feed fortnightly.

Growing
Cauliflower is a sensitive plant, more so than broccoli, so you'll need to keep the nutrients up and water

regularly. Make sure the soil drains by ensuring it is well-worked and not hard and clumpy.

Avoid planting cauliflower and broccoli in extreme heat, and cover the florets with leaves, a hessian sack or a light cotton blanket if you're expecting frosts. If you're growing white cauliflower, keep the heads covered with large leaves (tie two large leaves in a knot) so the vegetable retains its white colour. This process of blocking the sun is called 'blanching', and it can also be used when growing celery to protect its delicate colour.

Never plant cauliflower or broccoli in the same site for two years running. They leech nutrients from the soil, so you'll need a gentle crop, such as carrots, to follow. Tomatoes and strawberries also struggle growing near any brassicas, so avoid planting in the same bed.

All brassica varieties love growing near Mediterranean herbs, such as rosemary, thyme, sage and mint, while you'll find that beans, potatoes, beetroot and onion are also useful companions.

Harvesting

Cauliflower is a slow-growing vegetable – depending on your climate, it can take three to five months to ripen for harvest. The head should be about the span of a large adult hand and the florets blemish-free and compact. If the florets start to separate, you know that they've been left on the plant for too long. Take the whole head, either by cutting at ground level, or pulling the entire plant out of the ground. Cauliflower will keep in the fridge for up to one week.

Broccoli takes a long time to develop flower heads, but you can adopt a 'cut and come again' approach once it does. Chop the heads off and the plant will produce some more relatively quickly if you keep watering the plant. You may get two to three cycles of florets from a single plant, depending on your soil quality.

Pests

Caterpillars and the white butterfly are the major problems for cauliflower and broccoli, especially when seedlings are young. Ask the kids to check the underside of leaves regularly for slugs and caterpillars,

which you can feed to the chickens (if you have any) or blast with a Chilli Spray (page 72) or Garlic Spray (page 107). Check for slugs and caterpillars in the morning, as pests can hide in the soil during the day.

Drizzle coffee grounds, eggshells or even prickly chestnut husks around the plants as snails and slugs hate the gritty and dry texture.

We often companion plant masses of sage around all brassicas, to deter white butterfly – garlic, celery and dill can also help. Filling the garden with nasturtiums and marigolds will help to keep aphids away.

As we often eat our vegetables straight from the garden, we tend not to use any herbicides or pesticides. A few holes on the vegetables' leaves bothers us less than a mouthful of chemicals.

Quick ways with cauliflower and broccoli

- Steam and eat florets drizzled with extra virgin olive oil, salt and freshly ground black pepper.
- Add to curries, soups and stir-fries to bulk out the vegetable (and vitamin) content.
- Bake in the oven with a white sauce for a warming winter side dish.
- Munch on the raw florets with a selection of homemade dips.

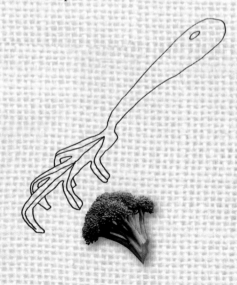

Cream of cauliflower soup

2–3 tablespoons olive oil

1 small brown onion, finely chopped

1 garlic clove, finely chopped

2 large potatoes, diced

½ head cauliflower, roughly
   chopped

4 cups chicken or vegetable stock

2 bay leaves

freshly ground black pepper

⅓ cup pouring cream

¼ teaspoon freshly grated nutmeg

Preparation time: 15 minutes
Cooking time: 35 minutes
Serves 4–6

This soup has a deliciously creamy texture. It is a perfect way to showcase a just-plucked cauliflower from the garden. If you can, use freshly grated nutmeg, as it adds a delicious depth of flavour.

Heat the oil in a heavy-based saucepan over medium heat and sauté the onion and garlic for 3–4 minutes, or until the onion softens. Add the potato and cauliflower to the pan and sauté for a further 3–4 minutes. Add the stock and bay leaves and season with freshly ground black pepper.

Increase the heat and bring to the boil, then reduce the heat to low and simmer, with the lid ajar, for 20 minutes, or until the potato is very soft. Remove the pan from the heat, discard the bay leaf and use a hand-held blender to purée the soup until smooth and velvety. Alternatively, transfer the soup to a food processor and pulse until smooth, then return to the pan. Return to the heat, stir through the cream and nutmeg, taste for seasoning and serve immediately.

 notes

If you like, make this soup in the early afternoon and let it sit for a few hours before reheating and serving – this will help the flavours settle and mature.

Kids love the smooth texture of this soup. It goes well with bread and butter and if you make your own stock, it's also super-healthy. This is important in the cooler months to keep the colds at bay.

If you want to freeze this soup, do so before adding the cream and nutmeg, which you can add once reheated. This soup should freeze for up to 1 month.

For a jazzed-up first course in the winter, serve this soup with warm crusty bread and a crumbly blue cheese scattered on the top, garnished with snipped chives.

Leek, bacon and potato soup

2 tablespoons olive oil

1 small onion, finely chopped

1 large leek, white part only, finely chopped

6 streaky bacon rashers, finely chopped

1 celery stalk, finely chopped

2 garlic cloves, finely chopped

4 large potatoes, finely chopped

1 bay leaf

1 handful finely chopped flat-leaf parsley

4 thyme sprigs, leaves removed and finely chopped

½ cup pouring cream

salt and freshly ground black pepper

Preparation time: 20 minutes
Cooking time: 1 hour
Serves 6

This is a family favourite that is thick and creamy and will satisfy even the heartiest of appetites.

Heat the oil in a large saucepan over medium heat and sauté the onion, leek, bacon, celery and garlic for 5–6 minutes, or until the onion is soft. Add the potato to the pan and sauté for 5 minutes.

Add 2 litres water, the bay leaf, parsley and thyme to the pan and simmer for 45 minutes, or until the potato is very soft.

Remove the pan from the heat, discard the bay leaf and use a hand-held blender to purée the soup until smooth and velvety. Alternatively, transfer the soup to a food processor and pulse until smooth, then return to the pan. Return to the heat, stir through the cream, taste for seasoning and serve immediately.

 note

For a richer flavour, substitute the water with the same amount of homemade or good-quality chicken stock.

Mediterranean chicken soup

1.2 kg whole chicken

3 tablespoons olive oil

1 large onion, finely chopped

3 garlic cloves, finely chopped

3 carrots, finely chopped

4 celery stalks, finely chopped

2 thyme sprigs, leaves removed

2 rosemary sprigs, leaves removed

salt

440 g can chopped tomatoes

1 bay leaf

2 cups finely chopped flat-leaf
    parsley

freshly ground black pepper

juice of 1 lemon

Preparation time: 30 minutes
Cooking time: 1 hour 40 minutes
Serves 6

This recipe highlights the versatility of the humble chicken – Asian one day, Mediterranean the next. Many cultures have their own version of chicken soup, believing the broth has incredible restorative powers – we tend to agree.

Remove and discard the skin from the chicken, then rinse and pat dry with paper towel.

Heat the olive oil in a large saucepan over low heat and sauté the onion, garlic, carrot and celery for 8–10 minutes, or until the vegetables soften.

Meanwhile, grind the rosemary and thyme leaves with ½ teaspoon salt into a paste in a mortar with a pestle. Add to the pan and sauté for a further 2 minutes.

Add the chicken to the pan with about 2 litres cold water to cover the ingredients. Add the tomatoes, bay leaf and half the parsley. Season with salt and freshly ground black pepper, partially cover with a lid and simmer for 1½ hours, skimming off any impurities with a large spoon, until the chicken falls easily off the bone.

Remove the chicken and, using tongs or a fork, pull as much meat off the carcass as possible. Return the meat to the soup, discarding the carcass. Discard the bay leaf. Add the remaining parsley and lemon juice to the pan, stir through and reheat before serving.

 note

You can create a tasty pasta dish with this leftover soup by adding 2–3 chopped tomatoes and extra shredded chicken (buy a pre-roasted 'chook' to cut corners). Add your favourite cooked pasta (penne works well) to the leftover soup and heat through well. Just before serving, add some freshly chopped herbs, such as flat-leaf parsley, mint or coriander, stir through grated lemon zest and top with grated parmesan cheese.

Tender lamb and pearl barley soup

3–4 tablespoons olive oil
2 onions, finely chopped
4 garlic cloves, finely chopped
2 carrots, finely chopped
3 celery stalks, finely chopped
6 lamb necks (or 4 lamb shanks)
salt and freshly ground black pepper
½ cup pearl barley
2 bay leaves

Preparation time: 15 minutes
Cooking time: 2 ½ –3 hours
Serves 6–8

This cure-all soup could well be penicillin for mothers everywhere!
It's also economical as it uses lamb neck, an inexpensive cut of meat.
The pearl barley stretches the soup – and the budget – even further.

Heat half the oil in a large, heavy-based saucepan over medium heat
and sauté the onion and garlic for 4–5 minutes, or until the onion is
soft and translucent. Add the carrot and celery to the pan and sauté
for a further 3–4 minutes. Transfer the mixture to a bowl and set aside.

Increase the heat to high, add the remaining oil and brown the lamb
on all sides, while seasoning with salt and freshly ground black
pepper. This will take about 8 minutes and you will need to turn the
lamb often to get an even browning off. You may need to do this in
batches to prevent over-crowding the pan.

Reduce the heat to low, return all the lamb to the pan with the sautéed
vegetables, pearl barley, bay leaves and 2 litres water. Partially
cover with a lid and simmer slowly for 2–2½ hours, skimming off any
impurities with a large spoon, until the meat is falling off the bone.
You may need to add a little water to the pan if the soup has reduced
too much. Discard the bay leaves.

Remove the lamb and, using tongs or a fork, pull as much meat off the
bones as possible. Return the meat to the soup, discarding the bones.
Adjust the seasoning to taste before serving.

Easy weeknight dinners

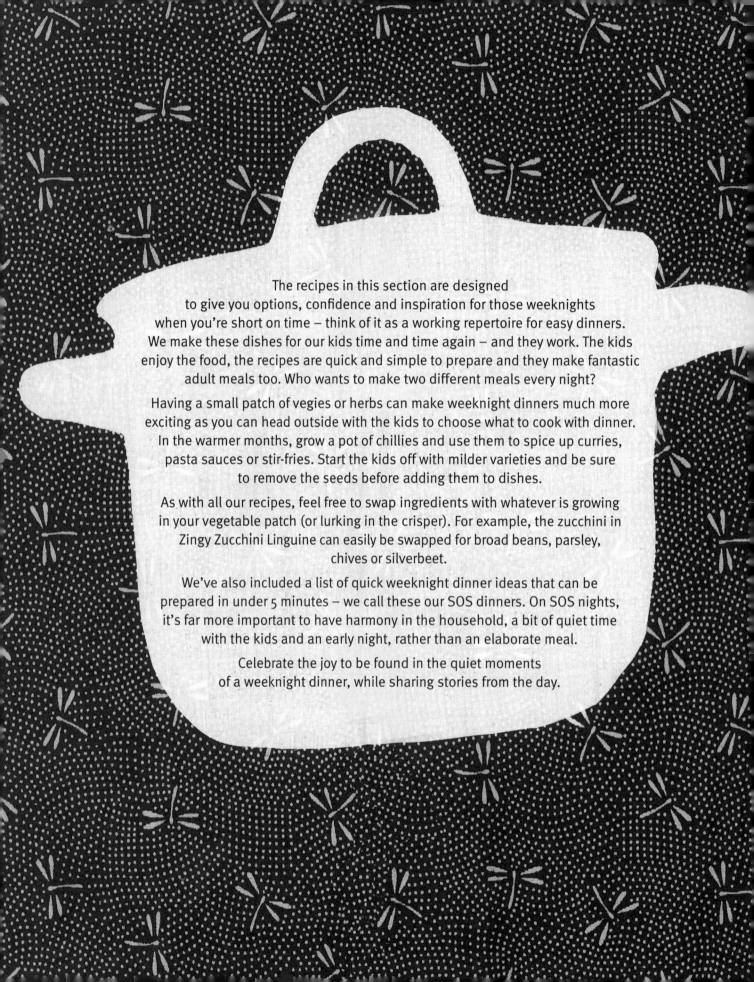

The recipes in this section are designed
to give you options, confidence and inspiration for those weeknights
when you're short on time – think of it as a working repertoire for easy dinners.
We make these dishes for our kids time and time again – and they work. The kids
enjoy the food, the recipes are quick and simple to prepare and they make fantastic
adult meals too. Who wants to make two different meals every night?

Having a small patch of vegies or herbs can make weeknight dinners much more
exciting as you can head outside with the kids to choose what to cook with dinner.
In the warmer months, grow a pot of chillies and use them to spice up curries,
pasta sauces or stir-fries. Start the kids off with milder varieties and be sure
to remove the seeds before adding them to dishes.

As with all our recipes, feel free to swap ingredients with whatever is growing
in your vegetable patch (or lurking in the crisper). For example, the zucchini in
Zingy Zucchini Linguine can easily be swapped for broad beans, parsley,
chives or silverbeet.

We've also included a list of quick weeknight dinner ideas that can be
prepared in under 5 minutes – we call these our SOS dinners. On SOS nights,
it's far more important to have harmony in the household, a bit of quiet time
with the kids and an early night, rather than an elaborate meal.

Celebrate the joy to be found in the quiet moments
of a weeknight dinner, while sharing stories from the day.

Quick pork and bean curry

2 tablespoons vegetable oil

1 onion, finely chopped

2 garlic cloves, finely chopped

450 g pork fillet, cut into 2 cm cubes

1 tablespoon mild curry powder

400 ml can coconut milk

1 large handful green beans, trimmed and cut into thirds on an angle

1 handful coriander leaves, roughly chopped

Preparation time: 15 minutes
Cooking time: 40 minutes
Serves 6

This curry is quick and easy – two words that parents always love to hear, especially during the week. Curries are a fantastic way to introduce new flavours to your kids. The beauty of this dish is that you can use any kind of meat – fish, beef, lamb or chicken – or even tofu for a tasty meat-free meal. Leave the coriander out if the kids don't like it, as it can be an acquired taste.

Heat the oil in a wok or saucepan over medium heat and sauté the onion and garlic for 2–3 minutes, or until the onion softens. Add the pork to the pan and sauté for 6–8 minutes over medium–high heat, or until the meat is sealed on all sides. Add the curry powder and stir well so that it coats the meat.

Add the coconut milk and simmer gently for about 20 minutes over low heat, or until the pork fillet is cooked through and the mixture has thickened. Add the beans and coriander and cook for a further 6–8 minutes, until the beans are tender. Serve with steamed rice.

 notes

To make a quick raita to cool down this curry, combine 1 cup plain yoghurt, ½ diced cucumber and 1 finely chopped garlic clove.

Serve this curry with an Asian-style salsa by combining ½ diced red onion, 1 cup chopped mint or coriander leaves (or both) and 2 cups chopped fruit, such as nectarines, peaches, mangoes, tomatoes or even fresh dates.

Sausage and risoni hot pot

3 tablespoons olive oil

1 onion, finely chopped

1 garlic clove, finely chopped

3 pork sausages

2 cups risoni or alphabet pasta

400 g can chopped tomatoes

10 pitted black olives

1 handful chopped curly or
    flat-leaf parsley

1–2 cups salt-reduced chicken stock

1 large handful green beans,
    trimmed and cut in half

grated parmesan cheese

Preparation time: 15 minutes
Cooking time: 40 minutes
Serves 4

Risoni, a rice-shaped pasta, is one of those ingredients that can be used in many different ways – and kids adore its size and texture. They'll also love this hot pot, which is simple to prepare and cuts a few nifty corners – such as squeezing the meat out of the sausage skins to make mini meatballs. If you don't have green beans to hand, good substitutes are peas, chopped zucchini or a few large handfuls of baby spinach leaves.

Heat the oil in a saucepan over medium heat and sauté the onion and garlic for 2–3 minutes, or until the onion softens. Cut down the sides of the sausages and squeeze the meat out of the skin into the pan, discarding the skin. Use a wooden spoon to break up the meat into mini meatballs as it cooks. Cook for 8–10 minutes, or until the sausage meat is completely cooked through.

Add the risoni to the pan and stir through the mixture to coat the pasta in the oil of the sausages. Add the tomatoes, olives, parsley and 1 cup stock. Cover with a lid and cook for 10–15 minutes, or until the pasta is *al dente* and the mixture is glossy and moist, adding more stock if the mixture becomes too dry.

Add the beans, reduce the heat to low and cook for 6–8 minutes, with the lid on, until the beans are tender. Serve with grated parmesan.

 note

Jazz up this dish a little by sautéing some chopped chilli with the garlic and onion and adding lots of fresh herbs, such as basil, oregano, marjoram or rocket, just before serving.

PEAS AND BEANS

Peas and beans are easy to plant, easy to grow and, best of all, it's easy to get the kids involved in growing and eating them. Grow your own and you'll never have to eat another awful bendy bean again. Kids also love shelling peas and broad beans for their dinner – keep an eye out to be sure you have some left for the meal!

The pea family includes the common garden variety, climbing or dwarf varieties and the sweet and tender snow peas and sugar snaps. All pea varieties are annuals, so they need to be planted every year.

The bean family includes runner beans, French beans and broad beans. Runner beans are perennial, but all beans do better when planted as annuals. The beauty of beans is that the flowers are so colourful, and you can collect everything from the perfect broad bean to the purple, scarlet, yellow, white and green runner beans. Keep an eye out for the spectacular heirloom varieties at your local nursery. For a bumper family crop, grow at least 4 plants per person.

Soil and site
Peas and beans like nutrient-rich soil that is well drained, toiled, composted and mulched. Do not over-water the soil, but make sure you water well once the plants have flowered and the pods are developing. Both peas and beans like exposure to the sun, and most varieties will need shelter from the wind and a support structure to climb.

Planting
Plant peas out in late autumn or winter while the temperature is still below 20°C but the soil is not lower than 10°C. Peas hate frosts, extreme cold and being in boggy soil.

Plant beans during the warmer months. You can start planting beans in mid spring (or at least a few weeks after the last frost) and keep planting through to late summer. We recommend avoiding planting at the height of summer.

Plant pea and bean seeds 5 cm deep, directly into garden beds or 50 cm pots. Get the kids to help plant the seeds, poking little holes with their fingers in which to place the seeds. Make sure the soil is moist when planting, but do not water too enthusiastically as the seeds will rot. Pots will need watering more regularly than garden beds and you should mulch both well.

Peas can suffer from transplant shock (like carrots) so it's best to plant seeds directly into where you want them to grow.

Peas and beans are easy to plant from seed and you get far more plants for your money than with seedlings. We recommend buying a few different varieties and swapping with friends or neighbours if you think you have too many seeds.

If you do buy seedlings, just make sure the central stems are strong and the leaves aren't yellowing. You need a strong, green plant to go into the garden.

Growing
Be careful not to over-water peas and beans. Once the flowers have emerged, lightly water the roots to ensure a good yield. Don't go overboard as they hate wet feet. You'll be picking beans within three to four months of planting, so we recommend staggering the planting of the seeds every fortnight so you have beans right through both growing seasons.

Peas and beans will need shelter and a structure to grow up against. Place supports for peas and beans in the soil before you plant, as this will avoid damaging the root systems. You can make a trellis out of wire, a teepee out of bamboo or old sticks and branches, or simply train the plants to grow up the side of a drainpipe, balcony, fence or wall. The kids will have a ball making teepees out of sticks and bits of string.

Beans, peas and potatoes tend to thrive when planted near each other. Each blocks the pests seeking the other. As beans and peas also fix nitrogen to the soil, they are excellent companions for all *brassicas* (such as cabbage, cauliflower and brussels sprouts), carrots, lettuces, spinach and silverbeet. In fact, we generally grow some kind of legume right through the year in all our garden beds and pots. They just keep giving back to the soil. When the season is finished, we just dig the whole plant back into the soil to make the most of all those nutrients. Avoid growing beans near onions, garlic and fennel, if possible, as they just inhibit growth.

Pests

Caterpillars, slugs and snails all like the tender seedling shoots of beans and peas so keep an eye out early on under the new leaves. Peas and beans are pretty hardy, so as long as you don't waterlog them they should be just fine.

Harvesting

Watch closely for when the plants flower. The pods will develop and be ready for picking about a fortnight after flowering. Pick as soon as the beans are ready. Regular harvesting will ensure more pods develop. Beans keep in the fridge for about three days before going bendy.

Store peas in the fridge in their pods and shell as needed. This will keep the peas tender and succulent.

Quick ways with peas and beans

- Steam or boil and coat with olive oil, sesame oil, soy sauce, or butter and pine nuts.
- Add to pasta, curries and stir-fries.
- Serve raw with dips.
- Sauté with other vegetables.
- Add to salads and side dishes for extra crunch.

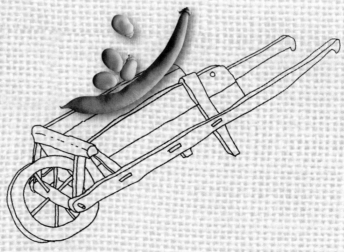

Vegetarian fried rice

3 tablespoons olive oil

½ onion, finely diced

1 garlic clove, finely chopped

2 celery stalks, finely diced

1 carrot, finely diced

2 cups cooked rice

1 small zucchini, finely diced

1 cup sugar snap peas, chopped

2 cups green beans, chopped

3–4 tablespoons soy sauce

1 tablespoon rice wine vinegar
   (optional)

Preparation time: 15 minutes
Cooking time: 10 minutes
Serves 4

This is a great meal for toddlers to start with – it's an easy dish to handle for kids with an 'L' plate on their cutlery. It's also very tasty and adaptable to any vegetable your kids are into. Try thinly sliced snow peas, shredded Asian greens, spinach or silverbeet, diced capsicum, bean shoots, sliced water chestnuts, asparagus, broccoli or cauliflower florets.

Heat half the oil in a wok or deep frying pan over medium heat and sauté the onion and garlic for 2–3 minutes, or until the onion softens. Add the celery and carrot and sauté for 3–4 minutes, until soft.

Add the remaining oil and cooked rice to the pan. Increase the heat to high and toss the rice and vegetables until the rice is separated. Add the zucchini, sugar snap peas, beans, soy sauce and rice wine vinegar if using. Toss the ingredients together for 2 minutes. Serve immediately (and relish the kids eating their vegies).

Crispy fish and potato rösti

1 cup rice flour
salt and freshly ground black pepper
500 g firm white fish fillets –
    we like flathead, blue grenadier
    or rockling
6 potatoes
1 egg
vegetable oil

Preparation time: 30 minutes
Cooking time: 15 minutes
Serves 4

This is a great way to get the family into fish – who can resist fried fish and crisp rösti? Rice flour creates a lovely crunch and a delicious taste, as well as being gluten-free, but feel free to substitute it for plain flour if you don't have rice flour to hand. Serve this dish with a garden salad and lots of lemon wedges.

Combine half the flour in a large bowl with 1 tablespoon salt and 1 teaspoon freshly ground black pepper. Dip each fish fillet into the seasoned flour, coat all over and set aside.

Grate the potatoes and place in a tea towel. Gently squeeze out the excess liquid from the potato, transfer to a bowl with the egg and remaining flour, and season with salt and freshly ground black pepper. Mix well and set aside.

It's important to cook the rösti and fish simultaneously, so you can serve this dish hot and crispy.

For the rösti, heat 2–3 tablespoons oil in a shallow frying pan over medium–high heat. For the fish, pour in enough oil to come 5 cm up the side of a deep frying pan over high heat. To check if the oil is hot enough, drop a small piece of potato into each pan – if it sizzles straight away, you are ready to go.

In the shallow frying pan, add enough potato mixture to form patties about the size of the palm of your hand (you may need to do this in batches). Fry for 4–5 minutes, or until the edges are golden. Carefully turn the rösti over with a spatula and cook for a further 3–4 minutes, until golden and crispy. The mixture should make about 8 rösti.

Meanwhile, in the deep frying pan add the fish, in batches, and cook for 2–3 minutes, until golden. Carefully turn the fish over and cook for a further 1–2 minutes, until golden and crispy.

Transfer the rösti and fish to crumpled paper towel to soak up the excess oil and season to taste. Serve with a green salad, lemon wedges and tartare sauce (see Note), if desired.

 note

Make your own tartare sauce combining ½ cup whole-egg mayonnaise, 1 tablespoon finely chopped capers, 10 chopped cornichons or 5 sweet gherkins and ¼ finely chopped red onion.

Quick Weeknight Dinners

Store-bought chicken with fresh salad

Baked potato with a mixture of toppings:
butter, grated cheese, chopped ham,
tomato, grated carrot, sour cream, chives

Grilled or pan-fried lamb chops, green beans
and new baby potatoes

Pasta with fresh chopped tomatoes, herbs,
Parmesan cheese and olive oil

Store-bought pizza bases with your choice of
toppings: tomato paste, ham, cheese,
rocket, capsicum and basil

Cheese on toast with chutney, served with a
bowl of cooked vegetables or salad on
the side!

Pasta with a can of tuna stirred through, olive
oil and fresh herbs

Scrambled eggs with peas, chopped tomatoes
and fresh herbs

Grilled chicken breasts with steamed rice
soy sauce and steamed bok choy or
spinach

Sweet potato and ricotta fritters with corn and capsicum salsa

1 whole garlic bulb

2 orange sweet potatoes (kumera), peeled and cut into 3–4 cm cubes

olive oil

salt and freshly ground pepper

1 cup plain flour

1 teaspoon baking powder

¾ cup ricotta cheese

2 eggs

¼ teaspoon freshly grated nutmeg

½ cup chopped coriander leaves

SALSA

2 corn cobs

½ green capsicum, finely chopped

½ red capsicum, finely chopped

½ cup chopped coriander leaves

½ red onion, finely chopped

2–3 tablespoon extra virgin olive oil

juice of 1 lemon

salt and freshly ground pepper

Preparation time: 10 minutes
Cooking time: 50 minutes
Makes 10–12 fritters

These fritters are light and fluffy on the inside and have a lovely crunch when you bite into them. Served with a corn and capsicum salsa and some fresh bread they make a hearty vegetarian meal. The recipe can be doubled easily and the mixture will keep in the fridge for a few days. You can then fry up batches whenever you need them.

Preheat the oven to 180°C. Cut the end off the garlic bulb so the tips of each clove are exposed. Drizzle the sweet potato and garlic with olive oil in a roasting tin and season with salt and freshly ground black pepper. Cook for 25–30 minutes, or until the sweet potato is soft and the garlic is easy to squeeze out. If the garlic needs longer, remove the sweet potato from the tin and cook the garlic for a further 10 minutes.

Meanwhile, for the salsa, slice the corn off the cob and combine the kernels with the remaining salsa ingredients in a bowl.

Squeeze out all the garlic and mash with the sweet potato in a large bowl. Add the flour, baking powder, ricotta, eggs, nutmeg and coriander and mix well. Season to taste.

Heat the oil left over from roasting in a non-stick frying pan over high heat (you may need to add a little more oil to the pan). Add tablespoons of the sweet potato mixture and fry each fritter for 3–4 minutes, or until golden and holding together. Gently turn over and fry for a further 2–3 minutes, until golden. Keep warm in a 100°C oven covered with foil until all the fritters are cooked. Serve with the salsa spooned over the top.

 note

Instead of the ricotta and coriander you could use crumbled feta cheese and thyme leaves for a more Mediterranean vibe.

CHILLIES

With chillies, think hot, hot, hot. Chillies need hot weather to grow – and are deliciously hot to eat. This is one plant where we advise really young children stay away from the planting, picking and slicing, as chillies will quickly draw tears if handled or eaten straight from the bush.

If you're cooking with chillies remember to wipe benches, boards and knives, and discard the seeds (to reduce its heat intensity), as chillies can burn. More than once we've had eager little hands help us in the garden and the kitchen, only to hear howls of agony as the chilli has made its way from little hands into little mouths and eyes.

So why bother with all this angst in a simple garden for families? Chillies take an ordinary pasta sauce and turn it into something sublime. Ditto for curries, stir-fries and soups. However, you do not need to sweat and have your tongue lashing about in a frenzy – you only need to add a small amount to create warmth and depth to any dish. It is this warmth that gives comfort to little (and big) tummies at the end of a busy day. The other reason we love chillies is that there are so many different types to choose from and they look divine sitting in pots around outdoor eating areas.

There are so many different varieties of chillies available, from the mellow banana chillies and spicy green jalapeño types from Mexico to the bright red and green bird's eye varieties from Thailand. Ask your local nursery for the best types for your climate.

If all else fails and you can't bring yourself to turn up the heat in any saucy summer dishes, then use your chillies as an effective garden spray to blitz caterpillars and other bugs (see recipe on page 72).

Soil and site

Generally speaking, if you can grow tomatoes then you can grow chillies. Chillies are creatures of the sun, and while they are biennial, they generally only last as an annual as they tend to die off once autumn hits.

Make sure you add manure or compost (or both) to your soil about six weeks before you plan to plant chillies.

Dig the fertiliser in well and let it break down because, like tomatoes, chillies like to suck the nutrients out of the soil. You can even use a specialist tomato fertiliser for chillies if you are ultra keen. We reassure ourselves with the thought that they run wild in countries such as Mexico and Thailand, so surely do not need too much nurturing. Just make sure you have the plants exposed to full sun in cooler climates.

Nurseries sell special grow-bags that are perfect for chillies. If you are planting seedlings into pots or hanging baskets, use premium grade potting mix, and mix some manure in six weeks prior just to give the soil a burst of nutrients. Manure isn't vital for chillies if you just plant straight into premium potting mix.

Planting

It is possible to grow chillies from seed, but frankly, half the growing season is over by the time they get going. Always anxious for that burst of colour and flavour, we tend to buy seedlings from our local nursery and put them in pretty pots near outdoor eating areas.

Growing

Like tomatoes, chillies like plenty of sun and water. The good news about chillies is that the more fruit you pick, the more you will grow.

Pests

You'd think an insect would be crazy to take on a chilli, but fruit flies love them. Basil grows well with chilli and also helps to keep the insects away. If you plant a Thai-style basil then you've already got half of a pretty good dish on your plate.

The good news is that chilli can be made into a spray and used to blitz many other bugs in the garden, particularly slugs, snails and caterpillars that eat up cabbage, lettuce, broccoli and cauliflower.

Harvesting

Watch out for the flowers because chillies will form quickly after this. The fruit won't really get going until the weather is consistently warm. Like beans, the more you pick, the more chillies will grow. The longer you leave fruit on the plant, the hotter and more intense the flavour will be – so pick early or when green if you prefer a milder heat.

Store chillies in a paper bag in the fridge for up to two weeks. For longer term storage, place whole chillies in an airtight jar, and keep in a cool, dark cupboard.

You can also hang and dry chillies in bunches and store long-term (six months or so). Use these chillies as dried flakes and seeds for curries and pasta dishes throughout the year. To make a hanging bunch, thread the chilli stalks with a needle – just make sure you wash your hands before touching your eyes and mouth, or wear rubber gloves. Dried chilli bunches also make good presents, so get busy when you've got a glut of the fiery fruit.

How to eat chillies

- Finely slice and stir through udon or vermicelli noodles in a lightly flavoured soup.
- Dice and add to any curry or pasta sauce.
- Sprinkle lightly over pizza.
- Finely slice and add to an Asian-style salad dressing.
- Dice and add to any to stir-fries.

Chilli spray

2 litre spray bottle

1 standard cake of natural soap, grated, or 10 ml liquid natural soap

8–10 small chillies (generally, the smaller the chilli, the more potent it is), finely diced

Fill the spray bottle with water and dissolve the soap in the water. Add the chilli to the soapy water and shake vigorously to combine. Spray this insect repellent on plants as needed.

Cheesy baked potato with chilli con carne

4 large potatoes (sebagos are good), unpeeled and scrubbed clean

2–3 tablespoons olive oil

1 onion, finely chopped

2 garlic cloves, finely chopped

1 red chilli, seeded and finely chopped

½ green capsicum, finely chopped

200 g beef mince

2 teaspoons ground cumin

400 g can chopped tomatoes

400 g can red kidney beans, drained and rinsed

1 knob of butter per potato

1 spoonful of sour cream per potato

2 cups grated cheddar cheese

Preparation time: 20 minutes
Cooking time: 1½ hours
Serves 4

Pop the potatoes in the oven when you get home from the school run and dinner will be ready at 6-ish without too much fuss. This is a delectably hot, buttery and cheesy dish for a quick weeknight dinner – especially on a cold winter's night.

Preheat the oven to 200°C. Prick the potatoes a few times with a skewer or fork and arrange in the middle of the oven directly on the rack. Cook for 1½ hours, or until the skin is crackling and brown.

Meanwhile, heat the oil in a saucepan over medium heat and sauté the onion, garlic, chilli and capsicum for about 5 minutes, or until soft. Add the mince to the pan, increase the heat to medium–high and sauté for 6–8 minutes, breaking up the meat with a wooden spoon, until browned and separated. Add the cumin and cook for a further 2–3 minutes, or until fragrant.

Add the tomatoes and beans to the pan, reduce the heat to medium and simmer uncovered, stirring occasionally, for about 30 minutes.

When the potatoes are cooked, cut a cross on the top of the potato and gently prise open. In the opening place a knob of butter, a spoonful of sour cream, a spoonful of the chilli con carne mixture and top with grated cheddar. Serve with a crisp green salad. The mince mixture will keep in the fridge for up to 4 days and can be reheated as needed.

Lemony lamb chops with baked vegies

1 onion, sliced

1 lemon, sliced

2 potatoes, thickly sliced

2 carrots, roughly chopped

2 tomatoes, roughly chopped

2 garlic cloves, unpeeled, bruised

8 forequarter lamb chops

2 bay leaves

2 rosemary sprigs

salt and freshly ground black pepper

2–3 tablespoons olive oil

juice of 1 lemon

Preparation time: 10 minutes
Cooking time: 35 minutes
Serves 4–6

We would almost class this recipe as an SOS dish – it tends to appear on our tables about once a week, especially in winter. If you're feeding a tribe, simply chop some more vegetables and add them to the baking dish.

Preheat the oven to 180°C. Arrange the onion and lemon slices over the base of a roasting tin followed by the potato, carrot and tomato. Top with the garlic and lamb chops then scatter over the bay leaves and rosemary sprigs. Season well with salt and freshly ground black pepper and drizzle with the oil and lemon juice.

Tightly cover with foil and bake for 25 minutes. Remove the foil and cook for a further 10 minutes, or until the chops are caramelised and the meat is falling off the bone. Serve with steamed green vegetables.

Weeknight spaghetti bolognese

2–3 tablespoons olive oil

1 onion, finely chopped

3 garlic cloves, finely chopped

500 g beef mince

2 celery stalks, finely chopped

1 carrot, grated

⅓ cup tomato paste

2 × 440 g cans diced tomatoes

3 bay leaves

2 handfuls chopped flat-leaf parsley

salt and freshly ground black pepper

500 g spaghetti

grated parmesan cheese

Preparation time: 20 minutes
Cooking time: 1 hour 15 minutes
Serves 8

If you ask our kids 'What's your favourite dinner?' they will always answer 'spaghetti bolognese'. This is one dish where you'll want to double the quantities and freeze some for an SOS night. The other great thing about bolognese is that you can grate or finely chop any unused vegetables and add them to the dish for a boost of extra nutrients. Any vegetable will work, so don't worry about the combination too much. We even add a can of lentils from time to time.

Heat the oil in a heavy-based saucepan over medium heat and sauté the onion and garlic for 2–3 minutes, or until the onion softens. Add the mince to the pan, increase the heat to medium–high and sauté, stirring constantly, for 8 minutes, or until cooked through. Use a wooden spoon to stir the meat and chop it up so it cooks evenly through the middle.

Add the celery and carrot to the pan, stir through the mince and cook for 2–3 minutes. Stir through the tomato paste and simmer for 2–3 minutes. Add the tomatoes, bay leaves and parsley. Season to taste. Reduce the temperature to low, partially cover with a lid and cook for about 1 hour, stirring occasionally.

Meanwhile, cook the pasta according to the packet instructions until *al dente*. Serve the pasta with the sauce, and parmesan cheese on the side.

Creamy bacon and vegetable pasta

3 tablespoons olive oil

6 streaky bacon rashers,
   finely chopped

1 garlic clove, finely chopped

½ small red onion, finely chopped

1 carrot, finely chopped

1 zucchini, finely chopped

1 cup frozen peas

3 silverbeet leaves, finely chopped

1 handful chopped flat-leaf parsley

250 g spaghettini

½ cup pouring cream

salt and freshly ground black pepper

grated parmesan cheese

Preparation time: 15 minutes
Cooking time: 15 minutes
Serves 4

This is one of our all-time favourite pasta dishes as it's quick and healthy. It's also a great choice for a kid's birthday party, where you could make it with kid-friendly fusilli (short curly pasta).

We often cook our pasta early for meals involving kids – it means you're not juggling multiple pans and busy kids in that mad hour before dinner. If you do cook the pasta early, drizzle it with a little olive oil to ensure it doesn't stick together and set it aside until needed.

Heat the oil in a heavy-based saucepan over medium heat and sauté the bacon, garlic and onion for 3–4 minutes, or until the onion softens. Add the carrot, zucchini, peas, silverbeet and parsley to the pan and sauté for 4–5 minutes, or until just soft.

Meanwhile, cook the pasta according to the packet instructions until *al dente*. Add the cooked pasta and cream to the bacon and vegetable mixture and stir through for 3–4 minutes, until well combined. Season with salt and freshly ground black pepper and serve with parmesan.

Roasted Mediterranean vegetables with lemony couscous

2 red capsicum, cut into
  3–4 cm pieces

2 green capsicum, cut into
  3–4 cm pieces

3 zucchini, cut into 3–4 cm pieces

1 large eggplant or 4–5 Japanese
  eggplants, cut into 3–4 cm pieces

2 red onions, cut into wedges

3–4 tomatoes, cut into wedges

6–7 garlic cloves, unpeeled

3 tablespoons olive oil

salt and freshly ground black pepper

HUMMUS SAUCE

1 cup store-bought hummus

1 cup Greek-style yoghurt

½ cup chopped mint leaves

juice of ½ lemon

½ teaspoon smoked paprika

LEMON COUSCOUS

2 cups couscous

juice of 1 ½ lemons

2 tablespoons olive oil

Preparation time: 20 minutes
Cooking time: 45 minutes
Serves 4–6

This dish is one of the most wonderful ways to use Mediterranean produce – capsicum, zucchini, eggplant, tomatoes – making the most of these vibrant, tasty vegetables. If you like, serve this dish with some barbecued pork or lamb fillets.

Preheat the oven to 200°C. Heat a large roasting tin in the oven. Combine the capsicum, zucchini, eggplant, onion, tomato and garlic in a large bowl with the oil. Season with salt and freshly ground black pepper and toss to coat well. Tip the vegetables into the hot pan and cook for 35–40 minutes, turning occasionally so they cook evenly on all sides.

Meanwhile, for the hummus sauce, combine the hummus, yoghurt, mint and lemon juice and set aside in the fridge. Just before serving, sprinkle the top with the smoked paprika.

For the lemon couscous, place the couscous in a bowl with the lemon juice and olive oil. Pour over 2 cups boiling water, mix well and cover with plastic wrap for 5–10 minutes.

Serve the roasted vegetables on a bed of the lemon couscous with the hummus sauce on the side.

ZUCCHINI

Zucchini get a bad wrap – ask kids if they like them and they'll often screw up their little faces. We would too if the only way we'd eaten zucchini was boiled until soft.

One of the best ways to eat zucchini is fresh from the garden, marinated in lemon juice and olive oil and grilled on the barbecue or grill plate. It's also delicious freshly grated over pasta with some garlic and chilli. If you have a bumper crop, you can enjoy zucchini all year round as they also make superb relishes and pickles – perfect too as presents.

The bright yellow flowers of zucchini are an amazing treat. Ask the kids to pick some, and stuff them with leftover risotto or a rice mix with some gooey cheese and fry them in a little olive oil for a snack that beats junk food any day of the week. They'll be blown away by both the novelty and flavour.

Soil and site

Zucchini is an adaptable plant that will grow almost anywhere. Just dig in compost or manure at least six weeks before planting so there are plenty of nutrients in the soil. The soil will also need plenty of drainage as zucchini roots hate being waterlogged. Zucchini prefers full sun, but will also grow in partial shade if you live in a hot climate.

Planting

Plant seeds straight into the ground in the warm months, but avoid the peak of summer. Ensure that any frosts have passed, or are not due to start, as zucchini will only thrive in the sun and warm soil.

Zucchini do not like being transplanted as their roots are shallow and can be damaged easily. This is why we recommend growing zucchini from seed if possible. Throw a couple in each hole and thin out the weaker plants. Plant about 1 cm into a raised mound of soil, and allow 1 m of spacing between plants as they ramble and need room. If you do decide to plant seedlings, first check the roots are not damaged or dried out, and the leaves are not yellowing or wilting.

Zucchini grows well in pots and looks lovely spilling over the edges of deep terracotta tubs or half wine barrels.

Growing

Zucchini likes plenty of water, so make sure the seeds are well watered to germinate. You may wish to add a complete fertiliser at the planting stage, but this isn't necessary if there is already compost or manure dug into the soil prior to planting. Give the plants another dose of fertiliser when they areis flowering to help the baby zucchini develop.

You may want to construct a mini tripod or some stakes for the leaves to climb up as they tend to sprawl everywhere. Get the kids involved in the construction.

Pests

Zucchini tend to be hardy but are prone to mildew if the leaves are too moist and the air doesn't circulate. Avoid wetting foliage and, like tomatoes, try to water down at the root zone.

Marigolds help ward off insects like aphids and we recommend planting some pretty companion flowers to fill any gaps in the vegetable bed. If you plant nasturtiums remember that they can spread up to 1 metre square. If kept unchecked they may crowd vegetables, preventing airflow and encouraging mildew.

Harvesting

Zucchini grow quickly. Aim for fruit about 10 cm long, and cut from the plant using scissors or a knife. Left to grow larger they will become tasteless marrows. Zucchini need to be harvested regularly to encourage more growth.

Zucchini keep in the fridge for a few days but tend to go mushy very quickly. Like all vegetables, they are best eaten on the day they are picked.

Quick ways with zucchini

- Stuff the flowers with a rice mixture, feta cheese or other vegetables and fry or bake.
- Cut into thin slices, drizzle with olive oil and grill, barbecue or bake.
- Grate or slice and add to pastas and stir-fries.
- Slice and add raw to salads.

Zingy zucchini linguine

500 g linguine

¾ cup extra virgin olive oil

1 large red onion, finely chopped

4 garlic cloves, finely chopped

2 red chillies, seeds removed and finely chopped

zest of 1 lemon

6–8 firm, young zucchini, grated

2 handfuls chopped flat-leaf parsley

salt and freshly ground black pepper

½ cup finely grated parmesan cheese

Preparation time: 15 minutes
Cooking time: 10 minutes
Serves 4

This is a light pasta dish that showcases zucchini's delicate flavour and beautiful green colour – perfect for the warmer months when the vegetable is in full bloom.

Cook the pasta according to the packet instructions until *al dente*.

Meanwhile, heat half the oil in a frying pan over medium heat and sauté the onion, garlic, chilli and lemon zest for 2–3 minutes, or until the onion is soft.

Add the zucchini to the pan and sauté for 3–4 minutes. Add the cooked pasta, parsley and the remaining oil. Stir through well and season with salt and freshly ground black pepper. Serve with the parmesan on the side.

 notes

For a zippier pasta dish add a handful of roughly chopped rocket leaves instead of the parsley – especially if you have this growing in the garden. Rocket has a terrific peppery flavour that complements the zucchini and chilli.

Instead of the parmesan cheese, a creamy goat's cheese or Persian feta cheese would add luxuriousness to this pasta dish. Fold crumbled cheese through the pasta right before serving, being careful not to break up the pieces too much.

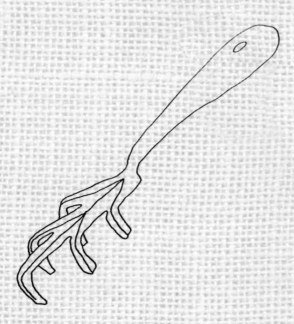

Chow mein noodles

2 tablespoons olive oil

1 onion, finely chopped

2 garlic cloves, finely chopped

400 g beef mince

1½ teaspoons Chinese
    five-spice powder

1 carrot, finely chopped

1 celery stalk, finely chopped

2 cups broccoli florets

85 g packet instant noodles, crushed

⅓ cup soy sauce, plus extra
    to taste

Preparation time: 10 minutes
Cooking time: 25 minutes
Serves 4–6

This is our version of sneaky weeknight takeaway food. It looks like the real deal but is packed full of vegetables and flavour – with no additives. Plus, putting it in noodle boxes is not only fun for the kids, but also saves on washing up! You can find noodle boxes at some supermarkets and party supply stores.

Heat the oil in a wok or deep saucepan over medium heat and sauté the onion and garlic for 2–3 minutes, or until the onion softens. Add the mince to the pan, increase the heat to medium–high and sauté for 8–10 minutes, breaking up the meat with a wooden spoon, until browned. Add the five-spice and cook for a further 2–3 minutes, or until fragrant.

Add the carrot, celery and broccoli to the pan and sauté for 5 minutes, until the vegetables are tender. Add the crushed noodles to the pan with ¾ cup water and the soy sauce and stir through. Reduce the heat to low, cover with a lid and cook for 4–5 minutes, or until the noodles are soft. Add more soy sauce if necessary and serve in takeaway boxes.

 note

If you want to jazz this meal up further for the grown ups, sauté some finely chopped chilli and ginger with the onion and garlic, and add a generous handful of chopped coriander leaves just before serving.

Sizzling Sichuan chicken

2 teaspoons Sichuan peppercorns
2 teaspoons sea salt
6 chicken thighs
2–3 tablespoons olive oil

Preparation time: 10 minutes
Cooking time: 10 minutes
Serves 6

We often make this dish for casual family barbecues. The first time we tried this recipe we made it for the adults, thinking the flavours would be too aromatic for the kids. How wrong we were – they barely left any for us!

Grind the peppercorns and salt in a mortar or spice grinder until very finely ground. Rub the mixture all over the chicken pieces, cover and refrigerate for at least 30 minutes, or up to 2 hours.

Heat the oil on a barbecue grill plate or in a char-grill pan over medium–high heat. Cook the chicken thighs for 2–3 minutes on each side, or until golden and cooked through. Take off the heat and let the chicken rest for 5 minutes under foil. Serve with steamed or fried rice and Sesame and Soy Snow Peas (page 152).

 note

Sichuan peppercorns can be found in the spice aisle of most large supermarkets. If you want, replace the peppercorns with a mixture of sea salt, black peppercorns and Chinese five-spice powder.

Tex–Mex tacos

2–3 tablespoons olive oil

1 onion, finely chopped

1 garlic clove, finely chopped

500 g beef mince or chicken thigh or breast fillet, cut into 2 cm slices

1 small green capsicum, finely chopped

2 tablespoons tomato paste

½ cucumber, diced

220 g sour cream

12 tacos or flour tortillas

½ iceberg lettuce, shredded

2 cups grated cheddar cheese

1 avocado, diced

TACO SPICE MIX

3½ tablespoons ground cumin

3½ tablespoons sweet paprika

2 tablespoons dried Italian herb mix

2 tablespoons dried onion

2 teaspoons salt

Preparation time: 15 minutes
Cooking time: 35 minutes
Serves 4

Mexican flavours offer a gentle foray into the spice world as they tend to be aromatic and mild. We have included a recipe for the taco seasoning. Commercial ones are available, but if your kids react badly to preservatives this is a great alternative. If you prefer, use flour tortillas to make fajitas instead of tacos.

For the spice mix, combine the ingredients in a bowl and store in an airtight container until needed. Makes approximately 1 cup.

Heat the oil in a large frying pan over medium heat and sauté the onion, garlic and 1½ tablespoons of the spice mix for 2–3 minutes, or until the onion softens and the spices are aromatic.

Add the mince or chicken to the pan and cook for 10–15 minutes, stirring often to separate the mince, until cooked through. Add the capsicum and sauté for a further 3–4 minutes. Add the tomato paste, stir through well, reduce the heat to low and simmer for 10 minutes.

Meanwhile, combine the cucumber and sour cream in a bowl and warm the tacos or tortillas as per the packet instructions. Arrange all the ingredients on the table and let everyone serve themselves.

 note

To make a quick tomato and mint salsa that goes perfectly with tacos and fajitas, combine 2–3 diced tomatoes, 1 handful of chopped mint leaves, ¼ finely diced red onion, 2–3 tablespoons extra virgin olive oil, the juice of 1 lemon and salt and freshly ground black pepper.

Tangy orange and hoisin pork

juice of 1 orange

2 tablespoons hoisin sauce

1 garlic clove, finely chopped

3 teaspoons sesame oil

500 g pork fillet

200 g udon noodles

2 tablespoons soy sauce

1 handul snow peas, finely sliced

1 handful roughly chopped coriander
leaves

Preparation time: 10 minutes
Cooking time: 25 minutes
Serves 6

Pork fillet is a wonderful, juicy cut of lean meat. The orange and hoisin sauce give this dish richness and, best of all, it is a quick and simple weeknight meal.

Combine the orange juice, hoisin sauce, garlic and 1 teaspoon sesame oil in a bowl. Lay the pork fillet in a shallow dish or bowl and pour the mixture over, tossing the pork to coat completely in the marinade. Cover with plastic wrap and marinate in the refrigerator for at least 30 minutes or up to 24 hours, stirring occasionally.

Heat a barbecue grill plate or char-grill pan to medium–high. Sear the pork fillet for 2–3 minutes on each side, or until the outside is browned and caramelised. Reduce the heat to medium and cook for a further 15–20 minutes, turning halfway through cooking. Remove the pork from the heat, cover with foil and let it rest for 5–10 minutes.

Meanwhile, cook the noodles according to the packet instructions. Drain and toss the noodles in a wok over high heat and stir through the soy sauce and remaining sesame oil. Add the snow peas and coriander leaves and toss to heat through.

Slice the pork on the diagonal and place on top of a mound of udon noodles. Serve with some steamed Asian greens on the side.

Sweet soy chicken

1 tablespoon honey
⅓ cup soy sauce
2 garlic cloves, crushed
8 chicken thighs, bone in

Preparation time: 15 minutes
Cooking time: 30 minutes
Serves 4

Chicken thighs with the bone in (sometimes known as chicken chops) are relatively inexpensive and easy to cook – especially in the oven or on the barbecue. Because the bone is left in, the chicken tends to stay juicy and tastes delicious. We often marinate double batches and keep it in the fridge for a couple of days so we can have this dish twice in one week. Just serve the chicken with different side dishes or vegetables to introduce variety.

Combine the honey, soy sauce and garlic in a bowl. Arrange the chicken pieces in a single layer in an ovenproof dish and pour over the marinade. Turn the chicken in the marinade to coat all over. Cover and set aside in the refrigerator, turning occasionally, for at least 30 minutes, or up to 2 hours.

Preheat the oven to 180°C. Cover the dish with foil and bake for 20 minutes. Remove the foil and bake for a further 5–8 minutes, turning at least once, until the chicken starts to become sticky and golden on all sides. Serve with steamed rice and green vegetables.

 note

For a simple side, sauté 1 crushed garlic clove, ½ cup chopped mushrooms and 2 chopped spring onions in a wok. After about 5 minutes, or when soft, add 4 cups roughly chopped Asian greens and 3 tablespoons oyster sauce. Cover the wok with a lid and steam for 3–4 minutes, or until cooked.

Slow cooking and weekend meals

Weekends are a time to
retreat, recharge and relax after a busy week.

We try to plan at least one meal a week where we sit
down together as a family. We often entertain family and
friends so some of these recipes are designed to be dished
up on platters for a crowd. A long, lazy lunch or an early extended-
family dinner are the perfect opportunities to offer new ingredients
and flavours to children.

When entertaining for large numbers you can't beat making your own
pizzas. You don't need a special pizza oven, just a barbecue with a
hood and a pizza stone, and you're in business. Add some beer, wine
and freshly squeezed juice for the young ones, keep everyone outside
and you have the perfect ingredients for a party.

For something a little more elaborate, take the time to shop for and
prepare special ingredients and recipes like fresh fish, gnocchi and curry
pastes. It's exciting to try new food flavours, and it's a real luxury
to have the time to potter about in the kitchen with the kids.

Weekends are also a good opportunity to spend an hour
or two in the garden, preparing the beds,
harvesting the produce
and planning
what to
plant
next.
Fertilising,
composting,
mulching
and weeding
are also key
weekend
jobs – and
many hands
(big and
small)
make
light work.

Pappardelle with broccoli pesto

500 g pappardelle

2–3 large heads broccoli, stems and florets roughly chopped

⅓ cup pine nuts

3–4 garlic cloves, chopped

2 cups grated parmesan cheese

3–4 oregano or marjoram sprigs, leaves roughly chopped, stems discarded

½ cup extra virgin olive oil

salt and freshly ground black pepper

300 ml pouring cream

Preparation time: 15 minutes
Cooking time: 15 minutes
Serves 4–6

This dish is a wonderful way to use broccoli – especially if you have a vegetable garden bursting with these *brassicas*.

Cook the pasta according to the packet instructions until *al dente*. Meanwhile, cook the broccoli in a saucepan of boiling water for 5 minutes, or until *al dente*. Drain and transfer three-quarters of the broccoli to a food processor with the pine nuts, garlic, parmesan and half the oregano or marjoram. Blend on low speed, adding the olive oil in a drizzle, until completely smooth. Season with salt and freshly ground black pepper.

Transfer the broccoli pesto to a saucepan over low heat and cook, stirring, for 5 minutes, until fragrant. Roughly chop the remaining broccoli and add to the pan with the cream, remaining oregano or marjoram and cooked pasta. Stir and heat through well before serving.

Teriyaki salmon with mushrooms and Asian greens

4 × 200 g salmon or ocean trout
  fillets, skin on

teriyaki sauce, to coat the fish

salt and freshly ground black pepper

2 cups sushi rice

1/3 cup rice vinegar

1 tablespoon caster sugar

3 tablespoons vegetable oil

2 cups mushrooms, such as shiitake
  or button, chopped

1 garlic clove, finely chopped

3 spring onions, finely chopped

3 stems choy sum, bok choy or
  broccollini, roughly chopped

Preparation time: 30 minutes
Cooking time: 35 minutes
Serves 4

This is one of those dishes that makes you look like a fantastic cook even though it's a breeze to create. This dish is also incredibly healthy and hearty – nobody will be left wanting.

Generously coat the salmon or ocean trout with the teriyaki sauce and season with salt and freshly ground black pepper. Cover and marinate in the refrigerator for about 30 minutes, until ready to cook.

Wash the rice in a colander under cold running water until the water runs clear. Drain the rice well by shaking it dry. Put the rice in a saucepan with a pinch of salt and 3 cups water and bring to a rolling boil over high heat. Reduce the heat to low, cover and cook for 12 minutes, or until the rice is cooked. Remove from the heat and let stand for 10 minutes.

Mix the rice vinegar, sugar and 1 teaspoon salt in a bowl until the sugar dissolves. Pour the vinegar mixture into the rice and stir with a vigorous cutting motion. The idea is to coat the rice with the mixture quickly and keep stirring to cool it down to room temperature. Cover and set aside until ready to serve.

Preheat the oven to 180°C. Heat half the oil in a frying pan over high heat and cook the fish, skin side down, for 3–4 minutes, or until the skin becomes crispy. Turn over and cook for a further 3 minutes. Transfer the fish to a baking tray, skin side up, and cook in the oven for 7–10 minutes, or until the flesh flakes easily.

Meanwhile, heat the remaining oil in a wok or frying pan over medium–high heat and sauté the mushrooms, garlic and spring onion for about 5 minutes. Add the Asian green stalks and cook for 1 minute. Add the leaves and cook for a further 2–3 minutes, or until glistening green. Serve the fish and vegetables with the rice and spoon over a little of the teriyaki sauce.

BROCCOLI +
CHINESE BROCC

ASIAN GREENS

Asian greens belong to the brassica family. Like their cousins, broccoli, cabbage and brussels sprouts, Asian greens are a healthy choice for the whole family, particularly pregnant women, as they are packed with important nutrients, including folate and vitamin C.

Asian greens can be steamed, stir-fried or added to salads. There are many varieties to choose from (and names can differ depending on where you shop), but our must-haves include: bok choy (or pak choy), which is a small Chinese cabbage perfect for stir-frying; wong bok (or Chinese cabbage), which is used in Korean kimchi or served raw in Asian coleslaws and salads; and tatsoi – tiny, dark green, spinach-like leaves with a thick white stem that are great for stir-fries and steaming.

Whatever variety you pick, no home garden is complete without a selection of leafy Asian greens – they are delicious, versatile and healthy, and can be tricked up to add flavour to the most humble of meals.

Soil and site

You'll need well-composted and fertilised soil with plenty of drainage – ultra-keen gardeners might also like to throw in a complete fertiliser before planting. Water regularly, but make sure the soil isn't boggy as you'll rot the roots of the plant.

Like all *brassicas*, Asian greens struggle in acid soil, so add a commercial lime solution two months before planting. Never stress the plant with too little water or nutrients in the soil as either the heads will not form properly or they will shoot straight to seed.

Planting

Plant Asian greens in the spring, late summer and autumn. Avoid planting in the height of summer or winter. Hot weather will cause the plant to struggle and they may go straight to seed, while heavy frosts will stunt their growth, if not kill the plants completely.

Plant in full sun – although if you're growing in the height of summer, you might like to plant Asian greens in the shade of corn, sunflowers or other taller plants. Asian greens are better sewn direct from seed. Like coriander, seedlings often turn yellow and struggle

once they've been transplanted. Get the kids to help you plant the seeds directly into the garden, about 30 cm apart and 5 cm deep. It's best to grow Asian greens in rows, and then thin out the plants that don't look healthy.

Asian greens are the perfect pot plant. Just throw the seeds into a half wine barrel, or a 30 cm deep pot filled with premium potting mix and some manure. The great thing about growing Asian greens in pots is that you can move them around to get the maximum sun in the different seasons, or protect them from the chill in winter if you plant them against a sunny wall. You can also keep the pots close to the kitchen for that last-minute side dish.

We tend to stagger the planting of Asian greens monthly, like lettuce, to ensure we have a continuous harvest right through the year.

Growing

Like all *brassicas*, the key to lovely, luscious Asian greens is to feed the soil long before you plant anything. You can use a complete fertiliser once the seeds have germinated.

Water regularly, but sparingly. Don't let the plants struggle for water – but don't flood them either.

Pests

Asian greens have the same pest problems as the rest of the brassica family. Caterpillars and white butterfly are the major problems, especially when seedlings are young. Get the kids to check the underside of leaves regularly for slugs and caterpillars.

Drizzle coffee grounds, eggshells or even prickly chestnut husks around the plants as snails and slugs hate the gritty texture and will stay away.

We often companion plant masses of sage around all *brassicas* to deter white butterfly. Garlic, celery and dill can also help to keep the pests away. Insects also hate blood and bone mixtures, so a layer of this over the garden bed can help keep the insects away.

Harvesting

Most Asian greens grow quickly and will be ready to eat within six to ten weeks of planting. Cut the entire head off at the base of the plant. Harvest in the morning as the leaves may wilt in hot weather.

Quick ways with Asian greens

- Steam and coat with sesame oil, tamari or soy sauce.
- Add to curries and stir-fries.
- Sauté with other vegetables.
- As a stand-alone side dish, sauté your preferred Asian greens with finely sliced garlic, spring onions and ginger.

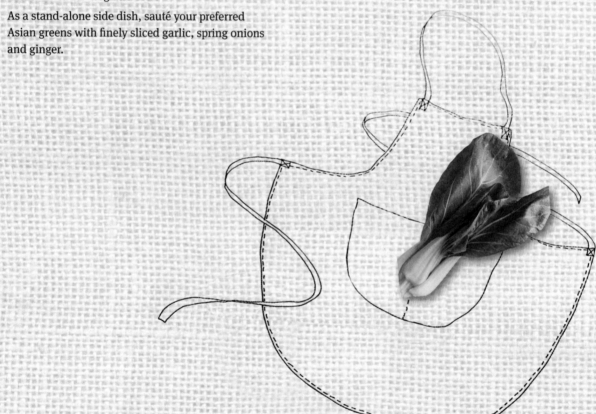

Sesame chicken vermicelli with Asian greens

2 teaspoons light sesame oil

3 tablespoons vegetable oil

3 spring onions, finely chopped

1 garlic clove, finely chopped

4 skinless chicken thigh fillets, cut into thin strips

1 x 250 g packets dried rice vermicelli noodles

12 snow peas, trimmed

2 bunches bok choy, roughly chopped

2 tablespoons soy sauce

Preparation time: 15 minutes
Cooking time: 25 minutes
Serves 6

This is a filling yet surprisingly light dish with plenty of greens and good hit of salty soy sauce.

Heat the sesame oil and 1 tablespoon vegetable oil in a saucepan or wok over medium heat and sauté the spring onion and garlic for 2–3 minutes, or until the onion softens. Add the chicken to the pan and sauté for 10–12 minutes, or until cooked through.

Meanwhile, soak the noodles in boiling water according to the packet instructions. Drain well in a colander, adding 1 tablespoon oil so they don't stick together. Add the noodles to the pan and if they seem too dry, another tablespoon of oil. Fry for 2–3 minutes, stirring constantly, until the noodles are well coated.

Add the snow peas, bok choy stems and soy sauce to the pan, increase the heat to high and cook, stirring constantly, for 2–3 minutes. Add the bok choy leaves and toss for 1 minute, ensuring the snow peas are still vibrant green and glossy, not soggy. Pile into large bowls and serve immediately with steamed rice.

Pan-fried veal with potato wedges

10 desiree potatoes, cut into wedges
100 ml olive oil
salt
6 veal scallopine (about 50 g each)
plain flour
20 g butter
lemon wedges

Preparation time: 15 minutes
Cooking time: 35 minutes
Serves 6

The simplest of meals are often the most rewarding. Choose good-quality ingredients and let them do the work.

Preheat the oven to 220°C. Place a baking tray in the oven to heat up. Cook the potato wedges in a saucepan of simmering water for 8 minutes, or until tender but still holding their shape. Drain and sit them in a colander until completely dry. Remove the baking tray from the oven, tip the potatoes onto the hot tray, drizzle with the oil and sprinkle over salt. Toss the wedges until evenly coated. Reduce the oven to 200°C and cook for 15–20 minutes, turning a few times during cooking, until golden and crunchy.

Meanwhile, lightly dust the veal in the flour. Heat the butter in a heavy-based frying pan over medium heat and when frothy add the veal in batches and cook for 3 minutes each side, or until golden. Transfer to paper towel to absorb excess oil. Repeat with the remaining veal. Serve the veal with the potato wedges and a green salad, with lemon wedges on the side.

Worcestershire steak

800 g skirt steak
2 garlic cloves, finely chopped
3 tablespoons Worcestershire sauce
3 tablespoons olive oil
salt and freshly ground black
    pepper, to season

Preparation time: 5 minutes
Cooking time: 15 minutes
Serves 6

Skirt steak is a cut of beef that marinates well, and because it's thin, it doesn't take long to cook. For steak, it's also easy on the budget. Serve with some boiled potatoes or steamed vegetables and a crisp green salad.

Marinate the steak in the combined ingredients for at least 4 hours, or overnight. This is an easy dish and works best barbecued on the grill plate, so juices can drop through. If you don't have a barbecue, use a char-grill or frying pan. It needs to cook for 5–8 minutes over high heat on each side. Then rest, covered with foil, for a further 5 minutes.

 note

Marinate the steak a day ahead and it will improve the flavour. However, the longer it marinates, the less cooking time it will need as the acidity in the sauce starts the cooking process. If you are pan-frying, make sure the marinade is completely drained off or the steak will stew in the juices.

Salt and Sichuan pepper squid

1 tablespoon Sichuan peppercorns

1 tablespoon sea salt flakes

½ cup plain flour

½ cup cornflour

4 cleaned squid tubes, about 20 cm in length

vegetable oil

lemon wedges

Preparation time: 20 minutes
Cooking time: 10 minutes
Serves 4

Contrary to what you might believe, squid is quick and easy to prepare. Ask the fishmonger to clean the squid, so you're ready to roll when you get home. Sichuan peppercorns are the X-factor ingredient – they have a unique flavour that is never forgotten.

Dry-fry the peppercorns in a frying pan over medium heat for 2–3 minutes, or until aromatic. Transfer to a mortar with half the sea salt flakes and pound with a pestle until finely ground.

Combine the flours and remaining sea salt in a bowl. Cut the squid into thin rings and toss in the flour until well coated. Set aside until ready to cook.

Pour in enough oil to come up 4 cm in a wok or large frying pan. Heat the oil over high heat until a cube of bread dropped in the oil browns in 15 seconds. Toss the squid rings in the seasoned flour a second time just before you drop them into the hot oil. This second seasoning makes them extra crispy.

Fry the squid, in batches, for 3–4 minutes, gently moving them around in the oil as they cook, until crisp and golden. Remove with a slotted spoon to paper towel to absorb the excess oil and transfer to a warm oven while cooking the remaining squid.

Sprinkle the cooked squid with the ground Sichuan pepper and salt and serve with lots of lemon wedges.

Barbecued pizzas

PIZZA DOUGH

2 teaspoons caster sugar

1¼ cups warm water

1 tablespoon (7 g sachet) instant
    yeast

500 g strong bread flour

½ tablespoon salt

pizza toppings of your choice (see
    page 102 for some ideas)

olive oil

*Preparation time: 1 hour (including
dough)*
Cooking time: 10 minutes
Makes 6 pizzas

Mention pizzas and the kids go wild! It will always be top of their list of fave foods – and they love to get involved. Invite a crew, get friends to bring different toppings and have a party. We suggest the barbecue because it gets everyone and everything outside – including the mess! You will need a barbecue with a lid and a pizza stone. Failing that use the oven, which still gets a great result.

Dissolve the sugar in the water then add the yeast. Cover with plastic wrap and let it sit for 5 minutes, until it has gone frothy. Put the flour and salt into the bowl of a food processor with the dough hook attached.

With the food processor on low speed, add the yeast and water mixture through the opening in the top. Increase the speed and mix until the dough forms a ball. At this point you can roll out the dough on a floured bench and knead for about 15 minutes, until it is smooth and elastic. Or, you can leave in the food processor for about 7 minutes on a medium speed until it is smooth and elastic. If the dough is too sticky, add a little more flour.

Lightly flour the dough with your hands and place in a large bowl. Cover with a floured tea towel and leave in a warm, draught-free place for 30–40 minutes, or until doubled in size.

Place a pizza stone on the grill and preheat the barbecue or oven to 220°C. Divide the dough into 6 balls. Roll out into circles about 1 cm thick and place one onto the hot pizza stone. Arrange the toppings on the pizza base and drizzle the edge with oil, to prevent it drying out. Replace the lid and cook for 6–8 minutes, or until crisp and bubbling. Repeat with the remaining bases.

Tasty Pizza Toppings

Layer tomato passata, ham, fresh
    pineapple and bocconcini

Layer tomato passata, garlic, bocconcini
sea salt, freshly ground black pepper
    and drizzle with extra virgin olive oil

Layer a base of olive oil, crushed garlic
and thyme with mushrooms and
    Teleggio cheese and rocket

Potato and rosemary

Rocket or silverbeet or chard and fetta

Cheese and garlic

Tomato, bocconcini and basil

Salami, olives and cheese

Caramelised onion and goat's cheese

Pumpkin, sage and blue cheese

Ricotta gnocchi with pumpkin and blue cheese

500 g butternut, kent or jap pumpkin

½ cup olive oil

500 g fresh ricotta cheese

½ cup finely grated parmesan cheese

2 eggs, lightly beaten

1 cup plain flour

⅓ whole nutmeg, finely grated

salt and freshly ground black pepper

1 small onion, finely chopped

1 garlic clove, finely chopped

1 cup pouring cream

200 g blue cheese, roughly chopped

flat-leaf parsley, thyme or marjoram leaves

Preparation time: 25 minutes
Cooking time: 1 hour
Serves 4

Gnocchi is a practical dish to serve a crowd as a little bit goes a long way and it lends itself to many different sauces.

Preheat the oven to 160°C. Peel and cut the pumpkin into 3 even pieces. Grate one piece and set aside. Cut the remaining pieces into 5 cm chunks and put in a baking dish. Drizzle with half the oil and bake, turning occasionally, for 20 minutes, or until soft.

Meanwhile, combine the ricotta, parmesan, eggs, flour, nutmeg, salt and freshly ground black pepper in a large bowl. Mix well into a dough then turn out onto a lightly floured work surface. Divide the mixture into 4 pieces. Roll each portion into a sausage shape about 15 cm long and 2 cm in diameter. Cut each sausage into 2 cm lengths and press a fork gently on one side to create ridges in the gnocchi. Transfer to a lightly floured board. Repeat with the remaining dough.

Cook the gnocchi in batches in a large saucepan of lightly salted boiling water for 4–5 minutes, or until the gnocchi rises to the surface. Remove with a slotted spoon and transfer to a small baking dish. Repeat with the remaining gnocchi.

Preheat the oven to 180°C. Heat the remaining oil in a large frying pan over medium heat and sauté the onion and garlic for 2–3 minutes, or until the onion softens. Add the grated pumpkin and sauté for 3–4 minutes. Add the cream and simmer gently for 5 minutes, or until it thickens. Pour the pumpkin and cream sauce over the gnocchi in the baking dish.

Dot the top of the gnocchi with the roasted pumpkin pieces and blue cheese. Season with freshly ground black pepper, cover with foil and bake for 15 minutes. Remove the foil and bake for a further 5–10 minutes, or until the top is golden and bubbling. Scatter with some freshly chopped herbs and serve immediately.

GARLIC

Nothing beats home-grown garlic – even the most expensive organic variety at the markets won't match the sweet aroma of garlic from your garden. The great news is that garlic does not take up a lot of room, and it stores really well, so it's possible to grow the household supply for the entire year.

Garlic makes a great companion plant around the garden so you can boost your plant numbers this way, rather than site them in a designated spot. You can plant garlic under roses to keep aphids away, under apple trees to prevent apple scab, near tomatoes to deter spiders and near peach trees to help prevent leaf curl. If you live in a mosquito-prone area, then a few garlic plants in pots can help keep the pesky insects at bay.

Garlic is also amazing at warding off colds and illnesses. If you live in a cool-climate area, add garlic to soups, marinades, curries, pastas and roasts right through winter to keep the dreaded lurgies at bay.

If you can find it, French garlic is a good choice. It is pink and has a sweeter, more pungent flavour than commercially grown white garlic.

Soil and site
Garlic needs a sunny spot with well-drained soil. If you have clay-based soil, plant garlic into mounds or ridges worked with plenty of organic matter so the garlic doesn't get too waterlogged.

Crop rotation is important for garlic so don't plant it in the same spot every year, as it is prone to fungal diseases in the soil. Also, don't plant garlic into the same soil following a crop of onions. Onions are heavy feeders, and may leave bugs and diseases in the soil, which can easily transfer to garlic.

Planting
Select and save the plump healthy cloves from a garlic bulb grown in the previous year, or buy healthy, disease-resistant stock from your nursery. We've even had success planting the cloves that have sprouted green shoots at the bottom of the cupboard.

Plant garlic at the end of autumn as, like all bulbs, they need a solid two months of cold weather in order to grow well. Avoid planting garlic near peas and beans, as together they will all fail to grow well.

Growing
Be careful not to over-water garlic. Garlic also benefits from companion planting with lettuce, chard, silverbeet and beetroot. The crop diversity helps to keep bugs at bay, and garlic benefits from having some friends around as it takes such a long time to grow.

Pests
There aren't too many pest problems for garlic – the main issue is getting the soil right and preventing fungal disease. Garlic is, however, an excellent deterrent for other insects and can be made into a potent brew to scare away caterpillars and slugs (see Garlic Spray recipe opposite).

Harvesting
Harvest garlic four to five months after planting. You can tell they are ready to harvest when the foliage starts to turn yellow. Once this occurs, don't leave them in the ground for too long as they will start to harden and dry out.

Dig up the plants carefully using a trowel or hand fork, so you don't damage the bulbs. Leave the bulbs to dry outside in the sun (if there is no rain) for a month, or dry on trays in a shed. Once the garlic is dry, clump together using the stems and hang, or plait the stems for an ornate garlic decoration. Kids love putting the garlic clumps together, and they make terrific home-made gifts.

Quick ways with garlic
- Preserve individual cloves and infuse olive oil by filling a jar with cloves, topping up with olive oil, adding a bay leaf and sealing.
- Roast whole garlic bulbs drizzled with olive oil and serve with a roast. Roasted garlic is also great cold on crusty bread the next day.
- Dice and add to curries and pasta sauces.
- Add to soups and pestos.

Garlic spray

3 garlic cloves, finely chopped
2 teaspoons vegetable oil
1 teaspoon dishwashing liquid

Soak the garlic in the oil for about 24 hours. Strain this mixture, discarding the garlic. Combine the garlic oil with the dishwashing liquid and 1 litre water in a large spray bottle. Shake the bottle vigorously and spray regularly for best results. Add diced chillies to be sure those caterpillars don't stand a chance.

Be aware: the mixture of oil and detergent can burn some plants. Always test the lower leaves of plants first to make sure they aren't affected. Use the spray in the cool of the evening so it does not burn the plant. Reapply if it rains.

Aromatic chicken with 20 cloves of garlic

2–3 tablespoons extra virgin olive oil
1 onion, roughly chopped
2 celery stalks, roughly chopped
2 carrots, roughly chopped
20 garlic cloves, unpeeled
1 large whole chicken
1 cup white wine
1 cup salt-reduced chicken stock
2–3 bay leaves
salt and freshly ground black pepper
1 large handful finely chopped flat-leaf parsley
1 lemon, cut into wedges

Preparation time: 20 minutes
Cooking time: 1 hour 20 minutes
Serves 6–8

This classic French-style casserole involves little preparation – you just let the ingredients and oven do the work for you while you focus on the family. This is a lovely meal served with some fresh crusty bread and a crisp salad. The garlic is left unpeeled and is delicious squeezed onto the bread.

Traditionally, this is a 40-clove dish, but we've prepared this recipe with young children in mind. As their palate matures, increase the number of garlic cloves and pretty soon you'll be wanting the full 40.

Preheat the oven to 180°C. Heat the oil in a heavy-based ovenproof saucepan or flameproof casserole dish over medium heat and sauté the onion, celery, carrot and garlic cloves for 3–4 minutes, or until the vegetables soften. Remove from the heat.

Place the chicken on top of the sautéed vegetables. Pour in the wine and stock, add the bay leaves and season well with salt and freshly ground black pepper. Cover with a tight-fitting lid and cook in the oven for 1–1¼ hours, or until the meat is falling off the bone.

Remove from the oven, sprinkle over the parsley and squeeze over the lemon, then let it sit with the lid on for 10 minutes before serving with crusty bread, green beans or a fresh green salad.

 note

If you have any leftovers, cook some pasta, drain and add some olive oil, salt and freshly ground black pepper. Pull all the chicken from the bone and add to a saucepan with the cooked pasta, any leftover sauce and a can of tomatoes. Simmer until hot enough to serve, then add fresh herbs, such as basil, chervil, parsley or rocket. Season well and serve with grated parmesan cheese.

Garlic prawn linguine

75 g butter

1 large red onion, finely chopped

4 garlic cloves, finely chopped

1 red chilli, seeded and finely
   chopped

30 raw prawns (about 250–300 g),
   peeled and deveined

1 cup white wine

500 g linguine

1 cup pouring cream

1 large bunch flat-leaf parsley,
   roughly chopped

salt and freshly ground black pepper

Preparation time: 20 minutes
Cooking time: 20 minutes
Serves 6

Seafood does not necessarily mean hard work – the ingredients in this dish do all the work for you. If you want to save more time, buy pre-peeled prawns.

Melt the butter in a heavy-based saucepan over medium heat and when frothy sauté the onion, garlic and chilli for 8 minutes, stirring occasionally, until the onion is soft and translucent. Add the prawns and sauté for 5 minutes, or until just turning pink. Remove the prawns and set aside. Try to leave in as much onion mixture as possible. Add the white wine to the onion mixture, increase the heat to high and cook for 8 minutes, or until reduced by half.

Meanwhile, cook the pasta according the packet directions until *al dente*. Add the pasta to the onion and wine reduction with the cooked prawns, cream and parsley. Stir well, season with salt and freshly ground black pepper and serve immediately.

 note

If you prefer to omit the cream, this dish can easily be adapted to an olive oil base. Use around 1 cup good-quality extra virgin olive oil instead of butter. This may seem like too much oil, but remember, you are replacing the cream. Essentially you will be making an olive oil 'sauce'. When you add the pasta and prawns back to the dish add more olive oil as needed to create a moist dish, rather than a dry sauce.

Crumbed lamb cutlets

2 eggs
3 tablespoons milk
1 cup flour
salt and freshly ground black pepper
12 lamb cutlets, Frenched
3–4 cups dry breadcrumbs
vegetable oil

Preparation time: 20 minutes
Cooking time: 10 minutes
Serves 6

Crumbed cutlets make a delicious spring dinner, but can be expensive when you buy them pre-crumbed from the butcher. Fortunately, it's so easy to create this dish in no time that it's sure to become a family favourite. Buy Frenched lamb cutlets as they are less messy to crumb when you have the bone to hold onto.

Mix the egg and milk in a bowl. Put the flour onto a plate and season with salt and freshly ground black pepper. Put the breadcrumbs onto another plate.

Coat the cutlets in the seasoned flour, dip into the egg mixture then press the lamb into the breadcrumbs to coat on all sides. Set aside and continue with the remainining cutlets.

Pour in enough oil to come about 1 cm up the sides of a heavy-based frying pan over medium–high heat. Test the oil by dropping in a cube of bread – the oil is hot enough if the bread sizzles and browns straight away. Add 3–4 cutlets at a time, making sure not to over-crowd the pan. Fry for 5 minutes each side, until crispy and golden. Transfer to paper towel to soak up any excess oil while you finish the other cutlets.

 note

For a variation on this dish, use loin chops and bake in a 180°C oven with a drizzle of olive oil for 30 minutes, turning at least once during cooking.

Lamb and rosemary pies

3 tablespoons olive oil, plus extra
  for greasing

1 onion, finely chopped

2 garlic cloves, finely chopped

1 carrot, finely chopped

1 potato, finely chopped

salt and freshly ground black pepper

500 g lamb shoulder, cut into
  1 cm cubes

leaves from 1 large rosemary sprig,
  finely chopped

40 g butter

1½ tablespoons plain flour

1 cup milk

⅓ cup beef or chicken stock
  (if the mixture is too dry)

5 sheets shortcrust pastry

5 sheets puff pastry

1 egg

1 tablespoon milk

Preparation time: 30 minutes
Cooking time: 45 minutes
Makes 8

Pies are the ultimate kids' party food – and a favourite snack for adults too. You can make them in advance and cook them when the kids come in from playing. Homemade pies are fresh and tasty – nothing like the flavourless stodge you get with store-bought pies. Make multiple quantities to feed a brood, or make pies on demand when you have lots of visitors through the house over the weekend.

Preheat the oven to 180°C. Grease 8 holes in a standard muffin tray. Heat half the oil in a frying pan over medium heat and sauté the onion and garlic for 2–3 minutes, or until the onion softens. Add the carrot and potato, season with salt and freshly ground black people and sauté for a further 3–4 minutes. Transfer to a large bowl and set aside.

Heat the remaining oil in the same frying pan and sauté the lamb for 6–8 minutes, until well browned. Add the rosemary to the pan, season with salt and freshly ground black pepper and cook for a further 6–8 minutes, or until the lamb is cooked through and tender. Transfer to the bowl with the cooked vegetables, stir to combine and set aside.

Melt the butter in a non-stick saucepan over medium heat and add the flour stirring constantly for 2 minutes until it forms a paste. Slowly add the milk and keep stirring for about 5 minutes, until it forms a thick paste. Remove from the heat and allow to cool slightly before stirring it through the meat and vegetable mixture. If the mixture seems too dry, add the stock, a few tablespoons at a time, until the consistency is like a thick gravy.

Cut out 8 circles from the shortcrust pastry to fit into the base and up the sides of the prepared muffin holes. Using your hands, gently mould the pastry into the muffin tins. Spoon a large tablespoon of the mixture into each mould – don't overfill or the pie will overflow. Cut out 8 smaller circles from the puff pastry to use as the pie tops. Press down the pastry and gently pinch the shortcrust pastry to the puff pastry. Whisk together the egg and milk and use the mixture to brush the tops of the pies. Transfer to the oven and cook for 20 minutes, or until golden and puffed.

If you prefer, these pies can be made in mini muffin trays to make 24 tiny pies. Simply reduce the cooking time to 10–15 minutes.

POTATOES

Potatoes are such a versatile vegetable – they can be decadent when served as a potato fritter topped with crème fraîche and smoked salmon, or the perfect comfort food when mashed with butter, milk and salt.

But with so many potato varieties available (and seemingly growing), it can be difficult to know which potato suits which dish – and which you should plant in your vegie patch.

In supermarkets, the most common varieties tend to be coliban and kennebec. Both are a floury, white potato with smooth skin, which mash and bake well. Serve floury potatoes mashed with lots of butter and milk to accompany rich casseroles. Or pick large ones and bake on a wire rack in the middle of the oven and serve as a winter lunch with butter or sour cream, grated cheese and spring onion.

Bintje is a waxy potato with brown skin and yellow flesh, which is good for boiling and serving with butter and chopped parsley or chives. Other waxy favourites include Dutch cream, desiree and nicola varieties.

One of our favourites is Tasmanian pink eye – a small, round potato known and adored for its sweetness. Try growing these at home as they are hard to find at markets outside Tasmania. They are best boiled, not mashed, and served simply with butter and salt.

The red-skinned, white-fleshed pontiac is a great all rounder – you can mash, fry, boil or bake it with great success. Another terrific all-purpose potato is the sebago, which is round to oval in shape, with white skin and flesh.

To get the kids' attention, try growing the oval-shaped purple Congo potato, which as the name suggests is a vibrant purple colour – it even retains its hue after cooking. It is best boiled and will have the kids oohing and ahing over its appearance. We can't say it enough: the more engaged your kids are in the process of growing and cooking food, the more willing they will be to try new flavours.

Another variety worth mentioning for its waxy character and beautiful yellow flesh is the kipfler potato. They are wonderful steamed and used in salads. Try steaming a bunch and making a traditional egg mayonnaise potato salad, throw in some bacon, finely chopped red onion and mint for a delightful accompaniment to any barbecue.

Growing your own potatoes is sure to delight everyone in the family – nothing can compare to the taste and satisfaction from a freshly dug potato, whichever way it's prepared.

Soil and site

Potatoes need a sunny aspect and well-drained soils. Make sure you keep potatoes covered with at least 10 cm of soil, as exposure to sunlight will turn the skins green and turn the plant poisonous. Potatoes can take up large tracts of a garden bed (each plant needs an area at least 50 cm x 50 cm wide). This is why we recommend planting potatoes in half wine barrels, or layers of car tyres to get maximum depth (and more potatoes) rather than a thin, spread-out crop.

Planting

Plant potatoes in spring once the frosts have finished. Frosts and temperatures below 10°C will cause the potatoes to struggle. In cool-climate areas you can plant potatoes right through until early summer. In warmer climates you can plant potatoes from autumn to winter, as they need temperatures of 15–25°C to thrive.

Purchase seed potatoes from your local nursery, or save some good ones from your crop the previous year. Most gardeners and horticulturalists advise against planting the potatoes that have sprouted at the bottom of the potato drawer (no matter how tempting for kids) because they often they carry viruses. Make sure you do not plant potatoes in the same patch of soil in consecutive years, and avoid planting tomatoes, chillies or capsicums within a year or two of planting potatoes, and vice versa. This will help to stop the spread of bad bugs in the soil.

Plant potatoes about 15 cm deep and add another layer of mulch about 10 cm deep. Once the green shoots come up and grow, layer up soil, mulch, hay or pea-straw around the shoot. You can build a layer up to about 70 cm as the shoots climb.

Some people prefer to plant their potatoes in car tyres, and add layers of tyres as the plants grow. Others chop the base off buckets, old plastic pots or garbage bins and build these up. Just make sure whatever container you choose has plenty of drainage. We have even had potato plants grow in our compost heap, having sprouted from potato peelings or offcuts.

Growing

Potatoes need plenty of water to thrive. It's important to keep building up layers of mulch and soil around the shoots to ensure you get the maximum yield. Some gardeners swear by sprinkling a layer of breakfast cereal, such as bran, between layers for extra nutrients.

Wherever we plant potatoes, we tend to plant peas and beans. The legumes feed the nitrogen back into the soil and keep those potatoes growing. Broad beans grow well with potatoes too – and also make a tasty combination in the kitchen.

Harvesting

Kids love harvesting potatoes – and getting dirty digging into the soil. Potatoes are ready for harvest once the green stem dies back. This should be within three to five months of planting the seed potato. It is possible to harvest potatoes before the stem dies, but they will be tiny. This early crop is referred to as 'new' potatoes.

Don't let the kids dig for potatoes with a shovel – they will inevitably chop them in half. Instead, dig carefully with a fork to loosen the soil, then use your hands to feel around for the potatoes. Ensure that the kids dig deep and wide, as there are multiple potatoes to a plant and you don't want to miss any.

You can keep potatoes in the ground, or a pile of sand if the temperatures are cool (below 10°C). We generally clear the refrigerator out and put the lot in for about three days to season them. This will stop them going green immediately. Once they've been given the instant cold snap, keep them in a cool, dark and dry area. Never wash potatoes if you are storing them (they'll rot if damp) and never expose them to sunlight as they will turn green and poisonous.

Pests

The most common problems for potatoes are viruses and bugs in the soil. These can generally be avoided by buying seed potatoes that are organically certified as virus-free and preparing the soil well in the first place. Good crop rotation is crucial – never plant potatoes in the same place in consecutive years and never plant potatoes in soil before or after tomatoes.

Quick ways with potatoes

- Boil and cover with olive oil, butter or fresh herbs from the garden.
- Mash – leave the skins on for maximum flavour and nutrients for your family.
- Bake with roasts.
- Thinly slice and layer with garlic, butter, stock and white wine.
- Bake whole with skin on and add toppings for an easy SOS dinner.

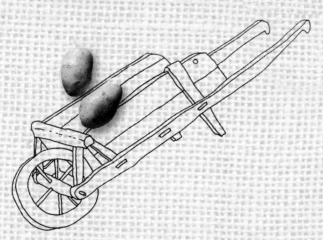

Beer-battered fish with thyme wedges

1 cup beer (sparkling ale is good)

1 cup self-raising flour

2 teaspoons sea salt, plus extra
  to season

vegetable oil

freshly ground black pepper

500 g firm white fish fillets, such
  as rockling or flake, cut into
  3 cm strips

lemon wedges

TARTARE SAUCE

1 cup whole-egg mayonnaise

1 tablespoon capers, finely chopped

8 cornichons, finely chopped

¼ red onion, finely chopped

POTATO WEDGES

10 desiree potatoes, unpeeled
  and cut into wedges

3–4 tablespoons olive oil

1 small handful thyme leaves

2 tablespoons sea salt

Preparation time: 25 minutes
Cooking time: 45 minutes
Serves 6

This recipe is all about the timing: read it through first and have everything prepared before you start cooking (you might want a mini helper). Fish, potato wedges, tartare sauce and lemon – you'll be very popular once you've mastered this dish!

For the tartare sauce, combine all the ingredients in a bowl, cover and set aside in the refrigerator until ready to serve.

For the wedges, cook the potato in a saucepan of lightly salted boiling water for 8–10 minutes, until just soft. Drain in a colander, then let them sit to dry out for at least 30 minutes. Preheat the oven to 200°C and heat up a baking tray.

Transfer the wedges to a bowl and, using your hands, mix through the oil, thyme and half the sea salt, ensuring the wedges are well coated. Tip the wedges straight onto the pre-heated tray. Cook for 30 minutes, turning occasionally and sprinkling with the remaining sea salt, until crispy and golden on the outside and soft and fluffy on the inside. The cooking time will vary, depending on the size of the wedges.

Meanwhile, mix the beer with three-quarters of the flour and the sea salt in a bowl until lump-free. Set aside at room temperature for 30 minutes.

Pour in enough oil to come about 10 cm up the sides of a deep frying pan and place over high heat. The oil is hot enough when a cube of bread dropped in the oil browns in 10 seconds.

Place the remaining flour on a plate and season with sea salt and freshly ground black pepper. Coat the fish strips completely in the seasoned flour. Quickly dip the floured fish into the beer batter, let any excess drip off and gently lower into the hot oil. Cook, turning gently in the oil, for 3–4 minutes, or until golden. Transfer to paper towel to absorb the excess oil. Repeat with the remaining fish. Serve the fish with the potato wedges, tartare sauce and lemon wedges on the side for squeezing over.

Thai green chicken curry

1 tablespoon vegetable oil

1 onion, finely diced

1 garlic clove, finely chopped

400 ml coconut milk

2 tablespoons fish sauce

1 tablespoon soft brown sugar

4 chicken marylands, skin removed

1 bunch bok choy, roughly chopped

2 tomatoes, roughly chopped

juice of 1 lime

1 cup roughly chopped Thai
basil leaves

THAI GREEN CURRY PASTE

1 bunch coriander leaves, stalks and
roots, roughly chopped

1 red onion, cut into quarters

4 garlic cloves

2 teaspoons ground cumin

2 teaspoons ground coriander

3 peppercorns, ground

1 teaspoon turmeric

1 long red chilli, seeded (leave the
seeds in for extra heat)

2 lemongrass stems, white part
only, chopped

1–2 tablespoons vegetable oil

Preparation time: 20 minutes
Cooking time: 45 minutes
Serves 4

This is not a traditional curry paste, in that we don't use whole spices and roast them. This is a 'realist' curry paste and we do cut corners. You can use store-bought paste if you like, but this simple homemade paste does deliver on flavour.

To make the curry paste, blend or pound all the ingredients except the oil together in a food processor or in a mortar with a pestle until smooth. Add the vegetable oil as needed to help smooth the paste. This paste will store in an airtight container in the refrigerator for 5 days or frozen for up to 3 months. Makes approximately 1 cup.

Heat the oil in a wok or deep frying pan over medium heat and sauté the onion and garlic for 2–3 minutes, or until the onion softens. Add all the curry paste to the pan and stir-fry for 2 minutes – this cooks the raw ingredients and releases the oil and aromatics in the spices.

Add the coconut milk, fish sauce and sugar. Bring to the boil for 2 minutes then add the chicken pieces. Reduce the heat to low and cook, partially covered, for 30–40 minutes, or until the flesh falls easily off the bone.

Just before serving, stir through the bok choy, tomato and lime juice. Taste for seasoning, adding extra fish sauce or lime juice if needed – try to balance the sweet, salty and sour flavours. Stir through the Thai basil and serve with steamed rice and raita.

 note

If you have kaffir lime leaves, add 2 leaves to the curry while cooking and shred another leaf to use as a garnish.

HERBS

Herbs can be grown in pots on windowsills or planted into gaps in any garden. We have herbs scattered under fruit trees and planted as companions right through the vegetable patches. Herbs grow best when they are alongside other herbs and vegetables rather than isolated, so plant them liberally throughout your garden as their foliage is magnificent, and the scent is as impressive as any ornamental flower.

If you like, you can make herbs the backbone of your garden. For aromatic and architectural effect, try repeat plantings of sage, rosemary, lavender and thyme for a low-maintenance, low-water garden.

Aside from their beauty, fresh herbs make the most simple dishes something special. Freshly chopped or torn herbs instantly transform any dish, such as baked or boiled potatoes, scrambled eggs, pasta and rice, and give zing to an ordinary green salad.

It can sometimes be difficult to get the kids to eat herbs as a garnish. But if you ask them to pick the herbs for dinner, pretty soon they will be begging you for 'sprinkles' to put over their food.

Growing

Work compost and manure into the soil at least six weeks before planting herbs. If you're planting into a pot, use a premium grade potting mix. All the herbs mentioned below will need well-drained soils and plenty of sun.

Perennial herbs that cope well with hot weather and limited water:

Bay: The fresh leaves are a must for casseroles, bolognese sauce and stews. Makes a fragrant hedge in sunny areas.

Chives: Chop and add as a garnish for salads and vegetables. Grows well near parsley; plant under apple trees to prevent apple scab.

Curry plant: Add to curry sauces for extra piquancy. Silver-grey foliage makes this an excellent border plant.

French tarragon: Survives tough weather extremes and adds depth to white sauces, roasts, casseroles and other slow-cooked dishes.

Lavender: Excellent companion for all vegetable and herb patches as the flowers draw in the bees. It also makes an attractive border plant. Lavender flowers can be crushed and combined with sage, thyme and rosemary for a Provençal-style rub for meats such as chicken and pork.

Oregano: Another hardy plant. Great for pizza toppings with mozzarella and anchovies, stirred through an omelette or scrambled eggs for that extra tang, or sprinkled over a bacon and vegetable pasta.

Rosemary: Thrives and looks majestic in most gardens with a minimum of care. Rosemary is a perfect match for lamb, chicken and roasted vegetables. We attended a talk once by British herb queen Jekka McVicar and she claimed rosemary tea is reputedly good for improving the memory. The tea can also be used to wash hair to make it shiny. She also suggested putting some rosemary in a vase where kids are studying, as it helps to increase alertness and memory. We think a vase of the herb in the kitchen for busy parents is a brilliant idea too.

Sage: This attractive herb goes well with pork dishes. Run fresh sage over teeth for instant shine. Sage makes a lovely perennial border in the garden and helps to keep white butterflies away from *brassicas*. A sage border can also help deter rabbits from taking over the vegetable patch.

Thyme: This aromatic herb invigorates most plants, and helps keep bugs away from cabbages and other *brassicas*. Perfect in slow-cooked pasta sauces and casseroles. Thyme is also fabulous in a chicken sandwich when soft, young leaves are chopped and mixed with mayonnaise.

Perennial herbs that need plenty of water:

Borage: Plant among strawberries to increase their sweetness. Use the blue flowers in ice cubes, or as an attractive garnish for salads. The blue flowers draw the bees into the garden.

Lemon verbena: Grab ½ cup of leaves and place in a teapot for a refreshing herbal tea. Allow to sit for 5 minutes before straining.

Mint: Contain mint in a tub or pot as it spreads easily. Separate different species of mint, such as Vietnamese, ginger and spearmint, as they cross-pollinate and end up losing their distinctive scents. Place a pot of mint under a well-used outdoor tap to catch dripping water.

Annuals that need to be planted every spring/summer (especially in cool climates) and need regular watering:

Basil: This herb is the perfect companion plant for tomatoes – in the garden and the kitchen.

Coriander: Needs regular harvesting and will bolt to seed in hot weather or if it struggles.

Dill: Perfect for fish and also mixed through mayonnaise for a simple salad dressing. Dill draws bees into the garden for pollination.

Parsley: Can be perennial, but hates cool weather so will die or struggle over winter if not in a sunny position and well tended. Parsley is a natural breath freshener – so munch on some after eating garlic or lots of pesto. Parsley is a great companion for tomatoes, as aphids hate it. Plant plenty for a thick border as you'll use it for everything.

'Best on ground' companion plants

Here's our quick pick of plants that should be grown in every vegetable garden to act as companions, repelling bad bugs and drawing good bugs in. They also look lovely.

Basil: repels insects.

Beans and peas: add nitrogen to the soil.

Borage: sweetens strawberries, the flowers attract bees.

Catmint: repels fleas, the flowers attract bees. Beware, as cats love to roll in catmint.

Comfrey: pest-repellent and yield booster for most plants.

Lavender: attracts bees to aid pollination.

Marigolds: deters a host of insects, including aphids and eel worm. Plant everywhere as a border plant.

Nasturtiums: deters a host of insects. Aphids hate orange nasturtiums. Good border plant, or garden-bed and pot-plant filler. Takes up to 1 square metre per plant, so allow some space for nasturtiums to sprawl.

Pyrethrum: pretty pest repellent, good border plant.

Sunflowers: kids love them, and they help shelter tender lettuce in summer. When sunflower seeds are ripe they attract the birds into the garden. You can also feed the seeds to your chooks.

Quick ways with herbs

- Tear the leaves and add basil, dill, parsley, chervil or chives to any green salad.

- Sprinkle coriander, mint, basil or parsley over diced red onion and tomato for quick salsa. Eat with fresh bread for a snack or serve as a side dish with curries.

- Sprinkle chopped coriander, curry or mint leaves over the top of curries to serve. Basil, particularly Thai basil, is great in Thai curries.

- Garnish your favourite pasta dish with fresh herbs.

- Dill is magic paired with fresh fish. Stir chopped dill through whole-egg mayonnaise as a lovely accompaniment to fish and chicken.

- Stuff a whole fish with coriander, lemongrass, chives, ginger and garlic, wrap in foil, and bake in a 180°C oven for 20 minutes.

Quick herb pesto

½ cup pine nuts

2 garlic cloves

½ cup extra virgin olive oil

1 firmly packed cup chopped basil,
  rocket, flat-leaf parsley or
  mint leaves

½ cup grated parmesan cheese

salt and freshly ground black pepper

olive oil

Preparation time: 10 minutes
Cooking time: 5 minutes
Makes about 1 cup

Traditionally pesto is made with basil, but we also make pesto when we have masses of rocket, parsley or mint in the garden. Best of all, you can easily double or triple the quantities – just adjust the olive oil and parmesan to get the consistency and taste to your liking. Use basil for rich, Italian flavours, rocket for a peppery pesto or parsley and mint for a bit of fresh summer zing. If you use a mortar and pestle, get the kids to help you pound away – they'll love it.

Dry-fry the pine nuts in a non-stick frying pan over medium heat for 2–3 minutes, or until lightly toasted and aromatic. Transfer the pine nuts to a food processor or mortar with the garlic, olive oil, herbs and half the parmesan and blend or pound until you have a thick, smooth paste. Season with salt and freshly ground black pepper to taste. Stir through the remaining parmesan and check the consistency. If it's too chunky, add a little more olive oil.

Spoon the pesto into sterilised jars (for instructions on sterilising jars, see page 186) and top with olive oil. If you plan on freezing the pesto, spoon portions into small sandwich bags and place directly into the freezer. Pesto will last for 2–3 weeks unopened in the fridge, 1 week opened, or up to 3 months in the freezer.

 note

For a zippy Asian-inspired pesto to add to curries or rice noodles, swap the pine nuts for peanuts, olive oil for peanut oil and use ½ cup coriander and ½ cup Thai basil. Add a small green chilli (or half a chilli if you want a milder one for the kids) and a splash of fish sauce to taste.

Instant mint sauce

1 cup chopped mint leaves

2 teaspoons sugar

1 tablespoon boiling water

½ cup white wine vinegar

Preparation time: 5 minutes
Cooking time: none
Makes about 1 cup

This is a simple sauce to whip up just before you dish up a roast lamb, or lamb chops. Our grandmothers would be proud.

Put the mint leaves and sugar in a jug and pour over the water. Stir until the sugar dissolves then add the vinegar. Stir just before serving.

Beef stroganoff

3 tablespoons olive oil

2 onions, thinly sliced

2 garlic cloves, finely chopped

50 g butter

2 cups button mushrooms,
   cut in half

1 kg gravy beef or oyster blade,
   cut into 2 cm cubes

salt and freshly ground black pepper

1 tablespoon tomato paste

2 tablespoons Worcestershire sauce

1 cup red wine

2 bay leaves

2 handfuls chopped flat-leaf parsley

½ cup sour cream

Preparation time: 15 minutes
Cooking time: 1 hour 20 minutes
Serves 6–8

This is a terrifically hearty winter dish. It is perfect for communal eating and goes particularly well with scalloped potatoes and wilted silverbeet or steamed greens.

Preheat the oven to 160°C. Heat 2 tablespoons of the oil in a heavy-based ovenproof saucepan or flameproof casserole dish over medium heat and sauté the onion and garlic for 2–3 minutes, or until the onion softens. Add the butter to the pan and when frothy, add the mushroom and sauté 5–8 minutes, or until glossy. Transfer the mushroom mixture to a bowl.

Season the beef well with salt and freshly ground black pepper. Heat the remaining oil in the same pan over medium heat and sauté the beef for 3–4 minutes, or until well browned. Add the tomato paste and Worcestershire sauce to the pan, mix through and sauté for 2–3 minutes. Return the mushroom mixture back to the pan. Add the wine, bay leaves and half the parsley with 1 cup water. Stir through well, cover with a lid and cook, in the middle rack of the oven, for 1 hour, or until the meat is tender. Just before serving, add the sour cream and the remaining parsley and stir through well.

 note

If you want to fast-track this recipe, use eye fillet, and instead of placing the dish in the oven, continue cooking for 20 minutes on the stove over a low heat.

Moroccan-style lamb with preserved lemon

3 garlic cloves

1 teaspoon salt

2 preserved lemon quarters,
  roughly chopped

2–3 tablespoons extra virgin
  olive oil

2 teaspoons ground cumin

freshly ground black pepper

1.2 kg lamb fillet

coriander sprigs

lemon wedges

Preparation time: 10 minutes
Cooking time: 25 minutes
Serves 6

This dish is a great weekend entertainer – it looks and tastes stunning without too much effort. Marinate the lamb on a Friday night and whip it out an hour before cooking on the Saturday. Serve with some crisp potatoes and a green salad.

Pound the garlic and salt in a mortar with a pestle until it forms a paste. Add the preserved lemon, oil, cumin and freshly ground black pepper and pound into a paste.

Coat the lamb generously in the paste and marinate in the refrigerator for at least 2 hours, or up to 24 hours. Bring the lamb back to room temperature before cooking.

Heat a barbecue hotplate or a char-grill pan to high. Sear the lamb on each side for 2–3 minutes, or until sealed and browned. Reduce the heat to medium and cook for a further 10–15 minutes if you like your lamb pink or 15–20 minutes for medium, turning occasionally.

Remove from the heat, cover tightly with foil and let the meat rest for 10 minutes before slicing and serving with coriander sprigs and lemon wedges.

Baked snapper with ginger, garlic and soy

1 whole snapper (about 1 kg), gutted and scaled

4 spring onions, white and green parts separated and finely chopped

5 cm knob of ginger, sliced

4 garlic cloves, finely sliced

2 lemons, sliced, or 2 lemongrass stems, white part only, sliced

½ cup soy sauce

½ cup water

freshly ground black pepper

1 handful chopped coriander leaves

Preparation time: 5 minutes
Cooking time: 45 minutes
Serves 4

We are finding that fish is increasingly being served as the roast of the day, replacing the more traditional lamb or chicken. And why not? Fresh fish is light, healthy and a breeze to cook. Add a fish dish to your family's roast repertoire and you'll never look back.

Preheat the oven to 180°C. Make two deep incisions across the body of the snapper on both sides. Stuff the cavity and incisions with the spring onion whites, ginger and garlic. Arrange the lemon or lemongrass slices on the base of a large baking dish and sit the fish on top.

Pour the soy sauce over both sides of the fish, getting into the cavity and incisions, and pour the water straight into the baking tray. Season all over with freshly ground black pepper.

Cover the dish with foil and bake for 35 minutes. Remove the foil and cook for a further 10 minutes, turning halfway through so both sides are cooked, until the skin is crispy and golden and the flesh is cooked through. To check if the fish is cooked, the flesh should be white and moist and lift easily away from the bone. To serve, scatter over the spring onion greens and coriander.

 note

This recipe can be adapted to cook on the barbecue. Instead of placing the fish on top of the lemon or lemongrass slices, use this to stuff the cavity of the fish along with the rest of the ingredients. Cut two slashes diagonally across each side of the fish and drizzle the soy sauce evenly over both sides. Wrap the fish tightly in foil and cook as per the recipe. Remove the foil and carefully place the fish straight on the grill for a further 10 minutes to crispen the skin.

Salads and vegetables

This section is full of ideas and easy combinations to get everyone excited about salads and vegetable dishes.

Side dishes are an important part of every meal because they create balance. They also allow you to add different flavours, textures and colours – all of which are important when getting children to try new foods. Each child can take on a role preparing the family meal and pretty soon they'll want to make these dishes on their own. Experiment, find your family's favourites and they will soon become staples.

We generally plan our meals by breaking down the elements: meat or other protein, such as fish, and the salads or vegetables to match. We often end up choosing a simple meat dish that can be prepared ahead of the dinner-time rush and whiz up some quick, simple and nutritious side dishes. This allows you to take full advantage of whatever you're harvesting in your kitchen garden.

The key to the dishes in this section is to let the produce do the work – choose vibrant, seasonal vegetables and you can't go wrong.

Perfect green salad

6 large handfuls salad greens, such
  as rocket, curly endive, mizuna,
  beetroot tops, watercress, baby
  spinach or tatsoi
1 garlic clove
pinch of sea salt
2 tablespoons red wine vinegar
  or lemon juice
⅓ cup extra virgin olive oil
1 tablespoon pouring cream
  (optional)

Preparation time: 15 minutes
Cooking time: none
Serves 6

This salad is the perfect foil for any main course, especially in the warmer months when you want something light. It's really simple to keep some perpetual greens, such as rainbow chard, silverbeet, spinach and lettuce, going in your garden or in pots over the summer months so that you can put a bowl of salad together anytime.

Wash, dry and chill the salad leaves in the refrigerator for at least 30 minutes. Pound the garlic with the salt in a mortar with a pestle to form a paste. Add the vinegar or lemon juice and combine before adding the oil. Mix thoroughly until well combined. If you want a creamier dressing, add the cream and mix through.

Just before serving, pour the dressing over the salad leaves and toss through until all the leaves are well coated.

Middle Eastern tomato salad

4 large tomatoes, finely diced
¼ red onion
½ teaspoon ground cumin
½ teaspoon ground coriander
salt and freshly ground black pepper
3 tablespoons extra virgin olive oil
1 handful chopped coriander leaves
1 small piece of preserved lemon,
  finely chopped

Preparation time: 10 minutes
Cooking time: none
Serves 6

Tomatoes are a fantastic ingredient as they can successfully take on so many variations of flavour. Even better, kids seem happy to experiment with tomatoes, especially when they have grown their own. This dish is so versatile that it works with a curry, or alongside any barbecued meats.

Combine all the ingredients in a bowl and mix thoroughly. This salad can be made an hour or so ahead of the meal to let the flavours develop.

Watermelon, red onion and olive salad

1.5 kg wedge of watermelon, skin removed, cut into bite-sized pieces

¼ red onion, finely sliced

1 cup pitted black olives

2 tablespoons extra virgin olive oil

sea salt and freshly ground black pepper

Preparation time: 5 minutes
Cooking time: none
Serves 6–8

Kids love watermelon. The juicy pink flesh of the flavoursome fruit also brightens up any meal. This is an easy salad that takes no time to make and is perfect served with any barbecue dish.

Combine the watermelon, red onion and olives in a bowl. Drizzle with the oil and season lightly with sea salt and freshly ground black pepper. Gently mix with your hands and let the salad sit for about 5 minutes before serving.

CARROTS

You may be wondering why you would bother planting carrots when they're so cheap to buy. As you'll discover, growing your own carrots has its rewards – they're so sweet and tender you can just brush the dirt off and eat them raw in the garden. Also, kids love pulling them out of the ground – just make sure they don't go overboard and pull the lot out in one go!

You can grow carrots throughout the year and they make an excellent companion plant for the vegetable patch. Along with the traditional orange varieties, you can also grow purple carrots, mini golf-ball varieties and several heirloom types. We even pull out the carrots when they are very small, as big as toddler fingers, and add them whole to stews and casseroles as they just look so cute – especially when you pick a mix of all the different colours and varieties.

Soil and site

Add compost and manure to the soil at least six weeks before planting. Make sure the soil has been well dug over – if the soil is firm or clumpy the carrots won't be able to grow down and they'll become bumpy or split.

Planting

Carrots are the perfect crop to plant when you have gaps in the garden and the soil needs a bit of a rest, as they don't take up a lot of nutrients. This means you can plant carrots directly after plants that are nutrient intense, such as cabbage, broccoli, cauliflower, silverbeet, chard and potatoes.

Plant carrots along with peas, to add some nitrogen back into the soil.

Sew seeds 5 cm apart and in shallow trenches 1 cm deep. Place a couple of seeds in each hole to ensure maximum germination, and just thin out when they sprout. Water well to help germination.

There are now some seed tapes available on the market. They are super easy to use – just dig the trench, roll out the line of seed however long you wish, then backfill the trench. Voila! It saves thinning down the track, and ensures carrots aren't squashed as they grow.

Growing

Once the carrots have germinated, you'll need to thin out the plants. The ideal spacing is 10 cm for the larger varieties. Carrots will need space to grow and will not reach their peak if they are jammed tightly together. We like to interplant our carrots with leeks, onions, celery, coriander, chives and lettuce. None of these vegetables are too taxing on the soil, and they seem to thrive in each other's company.

Pests

Carrots don't have too many problems with pests. Companion planting carrots with herbs, such as coriander, chives and sage, can help deter carrot fly, while good soil care and crop rotation can keep the maggots of the tiny carrot fly at bay.

Quick ways with carrots

- Boil or steam, then coat in sesame oil, sesame seeds and coriander.
- Coat with olive oil and bake in the oven to create a delicious, chewy, caramelised carrot.
- Add as a base to stews and casseroles.
- Chop and add to stir-fries and curries.
- Grate and add to pasta sauces.
- Grate and add to salads, including Middle Eastern and Asian-style coleslaws.
- Cut into batons and serve raw with a variety of dips for a fantastic after-school snack.

Carrot and sultana salad

½ cup sultanas
5 carrots, grated
juice of 1 lemon
⅓ cup extra virgin olive oil
1 teaspoon ground cumin
½ teaspoon ground cinnamon
1 small handful chopped mint leaves
salt and freshly ground black pepper

Preparation time: 10 minutes
Cooking time: none
Serves 6

You may think this seems like a strange blend of flavours, but both kids and adults gobble this salad up. It's quick and easy, looks beautiful and never fails to please a crowd. It is definitely one of our 'pull a rabbit out of a hat' standbys.

Put the sultanas in a bowl and cover with boiling water. Steep for about 5 minutes, until they plump up, then drain well.

Combine the sultanas in a bowl with the remaining ingredients and mix thoroughly. Let the salad sit for about 30 minutes to allow the flavours to meld together.

 note

Instead of cumin and cinnamon, try 1 teaspoon ground coriander and ½ teaspoon garam masala.

Tabbouleh

1½ cups coarse cracked wheat

½ red onion, finely chopped

1 garlic clove, finely chopped

2 Lebanese cucumbers, finely chopped

4 large ripe tomatoes, finely chopped

1 handful chopped flat-leaf parsley

1 handful chopped mint leaves

½ teaspoon ground cinnamon

½ cup extra virgin olive oil

juice of 2 lemons

salt and freshly ground black pepper

Preparation time: 10 minutes
Cooking time: none
Serves 8

This Middle Eastern blend of cracked wheat, tomato, cucumber, parsley and mint is irresistibly good. Tabbouleh is a fuss-free way to provide fibre to the diet. This is a great salad to serve with grilled or barbecued meat, poultry or fish.

Soak the cracked wheat in cold water for 10 minutes. Drain in a colander lined with a tea towel. Use the tea towel to squeeze out all the excess water. This ensures the tabbouleh does not go soggy.

Combine the cracked wheat in a bowl with the remaining ingredients and mix well.

CELERY

Celery is another one of those vegetables that you may consider easier to buy at the supermarket or greengrocer. It certainly takes some dedication to grow celery annually, but you'll be able to enjoy the whole plant – leaves, seeds and stalks. Store-bought celery often has the texture of wet, crunchy cardboard and tastes bitter. Growing your own means you can cultivate a far tastier plant that you would swear is no relation to the commercially grown variety.

Celery makes an excellent companion plant for carrots and leeks. Also, the leafy tops of home-grown celery can be eaten like parsley in salads, and have a lovely and sweet flavour.

Soil and site

Add compost and manure, especially poultry manure, to the soil at least six weeks before planting. Make sure the soil has been well dug over – it needs to be toiled and loose as the roots are shallow. The perfect spot for celery is in a wet, boggy patch with partial shade.

Planting

Celery roots are quite shallow, so it can be a tricky vegetable to transplant. For this reason we choose to plant seedlings.

Celery likes a cool climate and cool nights to get that crunch factor happening. Avoid the extremes of winter though, as it hates frosts. Spring, early summer and autumn are the ideal planting times.

Seeds can take a long time to germinate and grow large enough – around 10 cm – for transplanting. Plant seeds into seedling trays at least four months before you plan to plant them out in the garden.

Growing

Like cucumber, celery needs plenty of watering to ensure the soil stays rich and fertile. If you let the plant dry out, the stalks will taste bitter and stringy. Celery tends to thrive near leek, as they both like rich manure, such as duck or pig.

Unless you specifically request 'non-blanching' seedlings from your nursery, you will need to cover your celery stalks for about ten days before you plan to harvest them. This means you need to block the stems from the sunlight so they whiten and remain juicy and tender. There are a few options for doing this: piling the soil up high around the stalks, as you do for leeks; wrapping cardboard or newspaper around the stalks; or cutting off the tops and bases of empty milk cartons and sitting them over the stems.

Pests

Celery doesn't have too many problems with pests. It makes a good companion plant for the *brassicas*, including cauliflower, cabbage, broccoli, brussels sprouts and Asian greens.

Harvesting

The great thing about growing your own celery is that you can just chop stems or leaves off as you need them. This prolongs the season of the plant. You should harvest early morning as celery is full of water and will become bendy and wilted on hot days. If you do harvest the whole plant, it should keep in the refrigerator for up to one week.

Quick ways with celery

- Serve celery sticks raw with dips.
- Dice and add as a base to stocks, soups, casseroles and stews.
- Include in the lunchbox as a healthy snack for kids.
- Use both stems and tops raw in salads.

Simple celery salad

4 celery stalks, thinly sliced on an angle, reserving the tops
2 baby fennel bulbs, thinly sliced
juice of 1 lemon
1/3 cup extra virgin olive oil
salt and freshly ground black pepper
1 small handful chervil sprigs
1 radicchio or curly endive

Preparation time: 10 minutes
Cooking time: none
Serves 6–8

Once again, we found ourselves asking: 'What are we going to do with all of this celery?' We grow it because we love its crunchiness and know how good it is for us, but we often fail to make it through the whole bunch. This salad combo actually came together from just pulling a few ingredients out of the garden for a last-minute dinner. We combined it with the leftover celery and the rest is history – it's now a family favourite. Happily, the combination is perfect and complements any grilled meat dish.

Toss the celery and fennel slices in a bowl with half the lemon juice and 2 tablespoons of the oil. Season with salt and freshly ground black pepper and set aside for 10 minutes to allow the flavours to infuse.

Add the remaining lemon juice to a salad bowl with a good pinch of salt and some freshly ground black pepper. Stir well until the salt dissolves, then add the remaining oil. Blend with a fork until the mixture has thickened and emulsified.

Pick off about 10 tender, light-coloured celery top leaves and add to the salad dressing with the chervil and radicchio or curly endive leaves. Using your hands, gently toss the ingredients together. Just before serving, toss through the reserved fennel and celery.

✳ note
If you can't find chervil use flat-leaf parsley and try to find small leaves. It's worth adding chervil to the herbs you grow in pots (or the garden) as it makes a great garnish and has a delicate aniseed flavour that goes well in salads.

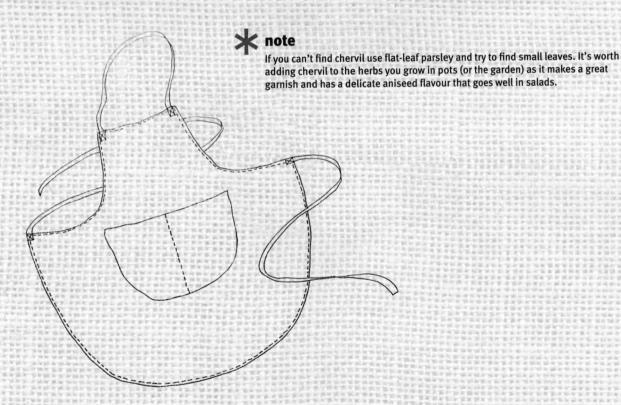

Tomato, celery top, bocconcini and caper salad

5 celery stalks, sliced, reserving
   the tops
¼ red onion, finely sliced
⅓ cup extra virgin olive oil
salt and freshly ground black pepper
8 tomatoes, cut into wedges (include
   cherry tomatoes if you have them)
8 large bocconcini balls, cut into
   quarters
⅓ cup salted capers, rinsed
   and drained
1 handful roughly chopped
   flat-leaf parsley

Preparation time: 15 minutes
Cooking time: none
Serves 6

If you keep celery in the fridge for a handy snack, then you'll probably be tossing out the tops. We did, until Peta came up with this tasty, crunchy salad. Soon you'll be buying celery just so you can make it.

Toss the celery and onion slices with 2 tablespoons of the oil in a large bowl and season with salt and freshly ground black pepper. Set aside to marinate for about 30 minutes, then add the tomato to the bowl and mix through.

In a separate bowl, toss the bocconcini with the capers and drizzle with 1 tablespoon of the oil. (Using separate bowls to prepare this salad may seem labour intensive, but it ensures the flavours don't dilute each other.) Season with salt and freshly ground black pepper and set aside.

Pinch off a small handful of the innermost leaves of the celery tops and roughly chop. Add the celery leaves and parsley to the tomato and celery mixture.

Combine the bocconcini and capers with the tomato and celery mixture and toss well to combine. Add the remaining oil and season to taste.

Silverbeet, cos and pickled onion salad

1 red onion, cut in half and thinly sliced

1 cup rock salt

juice of ½ lemon

pinch of caster sugar

salt and freshly ground black pepper

1 cos lettuce, shred into 2 cm thick slices

10 silverbeet leaves, shred into 2 cm thick slices

3 tablespoons extra virgin olive oil

2 tablespoons red wine vinegar

Preparation time: 10 minutes
Cooking time: none
Serves 4

This is an interesting salad as it sits for a while and the pickled onion and vinegar dressing softens the greens. The pickled flavour of the salad goes particularly well with Beef Stroganoff (page 123).

Put the onion in a colander and sprinkle with the rock salt. Toss to cover the onion evenly and leave to sit for about 30 minutes. Rinse under water until the salt is removed and pat dry.

Mix the onion in a bowl with the lemon juice, sugar, salt and freshly ground black pepper. Set aside for about 10 minutes to allow the flavours to infuse.

Toss the lettuce and silverbeet in a bowl with the onion mixture until well combined. Add the oil and red wine vinegar and toss through to completely cover the leaves. Taste for seasoning, adding more salt, freshly ground black pepper, oil and vinegar as needed.

Tomato and cannellini bean salad

**440 g can cannellini beans, drained
and rinsed**

4 large tomatoes, finely diced

1 small red onion, finely chopped

2 garlic cloves, finely chopped

1 handful finely chopped mint leaves

3 tablespoons extra virgin olive oil

juice of 2 lemons

**salt and freshly ground black
pepper**

Preparation time: 10 minutes
Cooking time: none
Serves 6–8

This recipe is so easy it could be an SOS lunch. Cannellini beans are a wonderful ingredient, and we always have a spare can or two in the cupboard.

Combine all the ingredients in a bowl and mix thoroughly. This salad can be made an hour or so ahead of the meal so that the flavours have time to deepen.

 note

Turn this into a side dish for a dinner party with a bit of extra flavour. Sauté the onion and garlic in olive oil first. Then add the tomatoes and beans and gently warm through. This is not a hot side dish, just warm, so add the chopped mint leaves a couple of minutes before serving. Serve in the middle of the plate with a piece of grilled fresh tuna on top and extra chopped mint leaves.

Spicy lentil salad

3 cups Puy or brown lentils

2 garlic cloves

3 bay leaves

½ cup extra virgin olive oil

juice of 1 lemon

½ red onion, finely chopped

1 large handful finely chopped
  coriander leaves

1 celery stalk, finely chopped

3 teaspoons ground cumin

3 teaspoons ground coriander

salt and freshly ground black pepper

Preparation time: 15 minutes
Cooking time: 30 minutes
Serves 8

Lentils are highly nutritious, cheap and simple to prepare, so they tick all the boxes for a family meal. Lentils can also feed a lot of people, so if you're having the whole clan over for a feast, this recipe won't break the bank. You can buy lentils in a can, pre-soaked, although they tend not to be as delicious as dried lentils. We like to use the pert little Puy lentils in this dish, but you can also use any type of brown lentil (other varieties will be too mushy).

Put the lentils, garlic and bay leaves in a saucepan, cover with water and bring to the boil over high heat. Reduce the heat to medium and simmer for 25–30 minutes, or until the lentils are soft. Drain, discard the bay leaves and cool completely.

Meanwhile, combine the remaining ingredients in a large bowl and mix well. Chop the reserved cooked garlic and add to the bowl along with the cooked lentils. Stir through well and check for seasoning. Cool in the refrigerator for about 10 minutes before serving.

CABBAGE

Nothing beats rows of green and purple cabbages jostling for attention in the garden. A vegetable patch feels incomplete without a few cabbages in the mix. They also look fabulous grown in deep pots or half wine barrels. Fresh cabbages are delicious, versatile and worth the extra effort feeding the soil and checking for caterpillars and bugs.

Soil and site

Cabbages need rich, well-composted and fertilised soil, with plenty of drainage. If you like, throw in a complete fertiliser before planting. Water regularly, but make sure the soil isn't boggy as you'll rot the plant. Cabbages, like other *brassicas*, do not like acid soil, so add a commercial lime solution 2 months before planting.

Never stress the plant with too little water or nutrients in the soil, as the heads will just grow warped and bobbly and even shoot straight to seed if they have to struggle. Avoid planting cabbage where it is exposed to extreme sun or frost. The plants tend to thrive if they are offered some shelter under taller plants, near fences or under hedges.

Planting

Cabbages hate extreme heat, so don't plant seeds or seedlings until the peak of summer has passed. Seeds sown in punnets will germinate in about a fortnight. Allow a month from germination for the plant to gain strength and then transplant to 10 cm pots and wait for seedlings to grow to about 10 cm before planting out in the garden. Alternatively, you can just plant three or four seeds in 10 cm pots from the outset and save this early transfer stage.

As always, leave the pots in the garden for a couple of hours each day to acclimatise before planting into beds. It's easiest to grow cabbages from seedlings purchased from the nursery. Just check all the leaves look strong and are not wilted or yellowing. Plant direct into the garden bed, give a complete fertiliser on planting and then fortnightly thereafter.

Growing

Like all *brassicas*, you'll need to keep the nutrients up, water regularly and make sure the soil drains. Avoid planting cabbage in extreme heat and cover the florets with cabbage leaves when you expect frosts, or even a hessian sack or light cotton baby blanket if you are expecting frosts for several days in a row. Aim to harvest your cauliflower within three to five months of planting.

Pests

Caterpillars and white butterfly are the major problems for cabbages, especially when seedlings are young. Check the underside of leaves regularly for slugs and caterpillars. For a non-toxic spray to blitz caterpillars and other bugs, try a homemade Chilli Spray (page 72) or Garlic Spray (page 107).

Drizzle coffee grounds, eggshells or even prickly chestnut husks around the plants as snails and slugs hate the gritty texture.

We often companion plant masses of sage around all *brassicas*, to deter white butterfly. Garlic, celery and dill can also help keep this pest away. Fill the gardens with nasturtiums and marigolds to help keep aphids away.

Quick ways with cabbage

- Shred and add raw to salads.
- As a filler for soups.
- Add to stir-fries, curries, soups and stews.
- Wilt the leaves and stuff with a spicy mince mixture and bake in tomato passata for 30 minutes.

Creamy cabbage and bacon

2 tablespoons olive oil

1 onion, finely sliced

1 garlic clove, finely sliced

2 bay leaves (fresh, if possible)

8 streaky bacon rashers, cut into
   1 cm strips

½ savoy cabbage, shredded

½ cup pouring cream

freshly ground black pepper

Preparation time: 10 minutes
Cooking time: 20 minutes
Serves 6–8

This is a wonderful winter side dish with plenty of oomph to go with roasts, especially pork and duck. Pretty soon your kids will be begging you for cabbage! If you want to dress the recipe up, pop in a teaspoon of ground allspice with the onion to add a delicious depth of flavour and to help complement the flavours of the main meat dish.

If brussels sprouts are thriving in your garden, you could easily substitute them for the cabbage in this recipe. Pull the leaves from 12 brussels sprouts, or just halve the tiny new ones from your garden, and sauté as you would the cabbage.

Heat the oil in a frying pan over medium heat and sauté the onion, garlic and bay leaves for 2–3 minutes, or until the onion softens. Add the bacon and cook for 8 minutes, or until cooked but not crispy.

Add the cabbage to the pan and sauté for 5–8 minutes, or until wilted. Add the cream, season with freshly ground black pepper and sauté for 2–3 minutes before serving.

Cheesy scalloped potatoes

2 tablespoons olive oil

6 carrots, grated

2 red onions, finely sliced

4 garlic cloves, finely sliced

8 large potatoes, finely sliced
  and patted dry

3 tablespoons finely chopped
  thyme leaves

2 cups grated parmesan cheese

salt and freshly ground black pepper

600 ml pouring cream

Preparation time: 30 minutes
Cooking time: 1 hour
Serves 6–8

Nobody seems to tire of this dish. It is rich in every way: texture, flavour and presentation.

Heat the oil in a saucepan over medium heat and sauté the carrot, onion and garlic for 8 minutes, or until the carrot softens. Remove from the heat and set aside.

Preheat the oven to 180°C. Cover the base of a 10 × 16 cm ovenproof dish with a layer of potato slices. Sprinkle with a little of the thyme and parmesan cheese and season lightly with salt and freshly ground black pepper. Repeat this layering until halfway up the dish (approximately 4 layers). Spread over the sautéed carrot and onion as the middle layer. Continue layering with the potato, thyme, parmesan, salt and freshly ground black pepper until finished.

Slowly pour the cream around the potatoes until it has all been absorbed. Cover with foil and bake for 45 minutes, or until the potatoes are cooked through. Remove the foil and cook for a further 5 minutes, or until golden brown. Allow to cool for about 5 minutes before serving.

Glazed baby carrots

1 large bunch of baby carrots
  (16–20 in total), trimmed but
  retaining some stalk

1 cup salt-reduced chicken stock

40 g butter

2 teaspoons sugar

salt and freshly ground black pepper

1 handful chopped flat-leaf parsley

Preparation time: 10 minutes
Cooking time: 10 minutes
Serves 4–6

This is an elegant way to serve carrots for a dinner party and is the perfect choice with roast lamb. Try these on the kids too – the sweetness will appeal to their palates.

Put the carrots, stock, butter, sugar, salt and freshly ground black pepper in a heavy-based frying pan and bring to the boil over high heat. Reduce the heat to medium and simmer for 8–10 minutes, or until the carrots are tender. Add more stock if the pan becomes too dry.

Transfer the carrots to a serving dish. If there is too much stock in the pan, increase the heat and cook the stock for 2–3 minutes further, until golden and syrupy. Pour the reduced stock over the carrots and scatter with the parsley.

 note

As well as baby carrots, look for the 'golf ball' varieties, which create a truly visual side dish – especially alongside baby turnips and baby golden beetroot.

Sautéed green beans

2 tablespoons olive oil
1 garlic clove, finely chopped
450 g green beans, trimmed
salt and freshly ground black pepper

Preparation time: 8 minutes
Cooking time: 8 minutes
Serves 6

Take advantage of green beans when they're at their seasonal best – there's so much you can do with them.

Heat the oil in a frying pan over medium heat and sauté the garlic for 2–3 minutes. Add the beans to the pan and sauté for 4–5 minutes, until glistening. Season with salt and freshly ground black pepper and serve immediately.

 note

For a flavoursome variation, sauté the garlic with 2–3 chopped prosciutto slices, 2 chopped tomatoes and ½ chopped red onion before adding the beans.

Sesame and soy snow peas

1 teaspoon sesame oil
2 tablespoons vegetable oil
400 g snow peas, trimmed
2 teaspoons soy sauce

Preparation time: 5 minutes
Cooking time: 8 minutes
Serves 6

The kids will love the crunch and flavour of this side dish. Snow peas are also really easy to grow in the garden or in balcony pots as they can just climb up a trellis, drainpipe or wall. Sugar snap peas also work well for this dish as they are plump and crunchy.

Heat both oils in a wok or frying pan over medium–high heat and stir-fry the snow peas for 4 minutes, or until glossy and still crisp. Add the soy sauce, turn off the heat and cover with a lid for 3–4 minutes before serving.

Pea and lettuce chiffonade

20 g butter

3 cups fresh peas (or defrosted if frozen)

1 iceberg or cos lettuce, finely shredded

salt and freshly ground black pepper

Preparation time: 5 minutes
Cooking time: 5 minutes
Serves 6–8

This dish is a flavoursome and attractive accompaniment to any roast dinner, especially a slow-cooked lamb dish. *Chiffon* means 'rags' in French, so *chiffonade* is the adjective used to describe the look of the lettuce once shredded.

Melt the butter in a frying pan over medium heat and when sizzling add the peas and sauté for 1–2 minutes. Add the lettuce and season with salt and freshly ground black pepper. Stir through until the lettuce is coated in the butter. Reduce the heat to low, cover with a lid and cook for 2–3 minutes, or until the lettuce is wilted. Serve immediately.

PUMPKIN

Pumpkins are one of the best vegetables to grow when you want to get children involved in the process. Kids love hunting under the large leaves of the sprawling plants for the earliest sign of the orange vegies. Then the competition is on for the next couple of months, as they inevitably choose their own pumpkin and wait to see which one will grow to be the biggest.

Pumpkins are relatively easy to grow. We've even heard of people who have had pumpkins growing and overflowing from their compost heap. The leftover seeds have gone in the compost, germinated, then thrived in the moist, nutrient-rich home. This must be one of the most attractive compost heaps around! Clearly pumpkins can thrive well on their own, given the right growing conditions.

Soil and site
Pumpkin tends to prefer slightly acid to neutral soil. Just dig in plenty of compost or manure at least six weeks before planting so there are lots of nutrients in the soil – pumpkins are heavy feeders and they suck it all up. The soil will need good drainage, so break up hard clumps because the roots hate being waterlogged, and you'll need to keep the water supply up for the pumpkins to grow successfully.

Pumpkins prefer full sun, but will grow in partial shade if you live in a hot climate.

Planting
Plant seed or seedlings straight into the ground in the warm months of spring and summer, avoiding the peak of summer. Be sure that any frosts have passed, or are not due to start, as pumpkins need the sun and warm soil to thrive.

Pumpkins need plenty of room to sprawl out with their big leaves and they tend to smother other plants nearby – good for killing weeds, but don't try to grow other vegetables underneath their reach.

You can grow smaller varieties of pumpkins in large pots, at least 50 cm x 50 cm, or half wine barrels. Pumpkins are great at covering unsightly mounds in the warm months – grow them over compost heaps, piles of dirt, piles of hay or mulch. As long as they have sun, food and water they'll be happy.

Growing
Pumpkins like plenty of water, so make sure the seeds are well watered to germinate and then right through the flowering and growing stage. You may wish to add a complete fertiliser at the planting stage, but this isn't necessary if there is plenty of compost or manure dug into the soil prior to planting. Top the garden bed with mulch so the fruit is not sitting directly on dirt. Pumpkins will start to rot if the fruit sits on moist soil. Give the plants another dose of fertiliser when flowering to help the fruit set.

Corn is the perfect companion plant for pumpkins. The corn protects the pumpkins from the height of the sun, while the pumpkins act as a mulch for the corn to retain water. Both love a good drink, so it's great to plant vegetables with the same water requirements in the same garden beds.

Avoid growing pumpkins near potatoes. Although they go well in a roasting tin, both plants grow poorly when sited alongside one another.

To have a go at growing a really big pumpkin (which the kids will love), pull all the other tiny fruit and flowers from the vine to channel the energy into just one fruit.

Pests
Pumpkins are a relatively trouble-free plant. You only need to keep an eye out for slugs, snails and caterpillars on the underside of leaves at the seedling stage and blitz them with a homemade Chilli Spray (page 72) or Garlic Spray (page 107).

Nasturtiums and marigolds help ward off insects such as aphids, and we recommend planting some pretty companion flowers such as these to fill the gaps in the garden bed as the leaves can sprawl out.

Harvesting
Pumpkins are ready for harvest when the foliage starts to yellow and die off, similar to potatoes and garlic, and when the skin starts to toughen up. This occurs in

late summer to early autumn. Make sure you harvest all the pumpkins before the frosts start.

Pick the fruit by cutting the stem about 5 cm from the base of the pumpkin. If you are planning on storing the pumpkins, you will first need to 'cure' them. This toughens the plant up for the long-term. To do this, leave the pumpkin out in the sun for at least a week, possibly a fortnight, to ensure it dries out. Store in a cool, dark place after curing for a couple of months. They should last almost six months, although they will start to become a little woody by then.

Quick ways with pumpkin

- Toast the seeds for a healthy snack and season with sesame oil, olive oil or spices like smoked paprika.
- Boil and serve as a traditional mash.
- Bake in the oven as part of a roast, or on its own.
- Make American-style pumpkin pies.
- Add to muffins along with corn and cumin.
- Slice finely and add to pizza toppings – pumpkin, blue cheese and rocket make a heavenly combo.
- Boil, then add stock, onion and garlic for the perfect pumpkin soup.

Asian-style butternut pumpkin

3 cm piece of ginger, finely chopped

1 tablespoon minced garlic

½ cup finely chopped coriander leaves

1 cup coconut milk

salt and freshly ground black pepper

½ large butternut pumpkin, seeds scooped out

Preparation time: 5 minutes
Cooking time: 1 hour
Serves 4–6

Cooking pumpkin like this creates the smoothest, most decadent result. It will become a much-loved dish that will happily accompany any meal. Play around with the stuffing ingredients to invent different flavour styles.

Preheat the oven to 190°C. Combine the ginger, garlic, coriander and coconut milk in a jug or bowl and season with salt and freshly ground black pepper. Pour the mixture into the pumpkin cavity and double wrap the entire pumpkin with foil.

Bake, cavity side up, for 45 minutes to 1 hour, or until the pumpkin flesh is tender when tested with a skewer. Serve the pumpkin in the foil at the table with a spoon to scoop out the flesh.

Sweet potato and garlic mash

5 orange sweet potatoes (kumera),
    peeled and cut into 4 cm-thick
    rounds
2 garlic bulbs, tops cut off
100 ml extra virgin olive oil
salt and freshly ground black pepper
1/3 finely ground whole nutmeg

Preparation time: 10 minutes
Cooking time: 30 minutes
Serves 4–6

The combination of roasted sweet potato and garlic is earthy and gutsy, and this side would go well with any meat dish. Serve it in a big white bowl to show off sweet potato's dazzling colour.

Preheat the oven to 180°C. Put the sweet potato and garlic in a roasting tin, drizzle with 2 tablespoons of the oil and season with salt and freshly ground black pepper. Give the tin a good shake so all the sweet potato slices are well coated with the oil.

Roast for 20 minutes, turning occasionally. Sweet potato often cooks more quickly than garlic, so if the potatoes are soft enough to mash with a fork, take them out to cool while the garlic finishes cooking.

Mash the sweet potato while still hot with the remaining oil and nutmeg and season with salt and freshly ground black pepper. When the garlic has cooked, squeeze out the roasted cloves and mix it into the sweet potato mash.

Simple mashed potato

6 floury potatoes, such as coliban,
    Dutch cream or nicola, peeled and
    cut into quarters
1/2 cup hot milk
1 tablespoon butter
salt and freshly ground black pepper

Preparation time: 10 minutes
Cooking time: 15 minutes
Serves 4–6

Mashed potato, mashed potato – it seems the Wiggles know the secret! There is no better accompaniment to any meal than mashed potato. Sausages and mash, chops and mash, any casserole and mash – the list is endless. To dress up this classic, stir through a handful of freshly chopped flat-leaf parsley or chives before serving.

Cook the potatoes in a saucepan of boiling water for 15 minutes, or until tender. Drain and roughly mash in the same saucepan.

Meanwhile, heat the milk and butter in a separate saucepan over medium heat until the butter melts. Pour the mixture gradually over the potatoes and mash until smooth and creamy. Season with salt and freshly ground black pepper and serve.

Sweet treats

It's a rare child who doesn't look forward to a sweet treat (and a rare adult in our household!) – and the excitement is tenfold if you've picked the ingredients straight from the garden. In this section we talk about growing strawberries – which you can do in a hanging basket on a balcony – as well as rhubarb, for some truly knockout desserts. The intensity of flavour of home grown strawberries and rhubarb is unbeatable.

This is a collection of sweet treats that are both yummy and reliable. You'll meet old friends like Golden Syrup Dumplings, Nutty Ice Cream Sundaes, gooey Lemon Delicious Pudding and Quick Berry Trifles. Some are quick weeknight treats and others are a bit more involved – but all will incite 'oohs and aahs' at the table. And, for an afternoon tea or lunchbox treat, you can't beat the decadent Banana and Chocolate Cake.

Chances are you won't be whipping up a dessert every night. For six out of the seven nights of the week, our kids usually get fruit, or fruit and plain yoghurt, so these recipes are designed for those special evenings. We have also included a list of our top 10 quick desserts for when time is short and a little sweetness is a high priority.

Lemon delicious pudding

20 g unsalted butter

1 cup caster sugar

juice of 1 lemon

finely grated zest of 2 lemons

3 eggs, separated

1½ tablespoons self-raising flour

1¼ cups milk

Preparation time: 20 minutes
Cooking time: 45 minutes
Serves 6

Lemon delicious pudding is an old-fashioned classic that deserves a place in every family cookbook.

Preheat the oven to 180°C. Grease a 2 litre ovenproof bowl. Beat the butter and sugar with a wooden spoon or electric beaters until creamy. Add the lemon juice, lemon zest and egg yolks and stir until just combined. Add the flour and milk gradually, beating between each addition, until combined.

In a separate bowl, beat the egg whites with electric beaters until stiff peaks form. Gently fold the egg whites into the batter mixture using a cutting motion through the middle. Combine well but gently, taking care to keep the mixture light and airy.

Pour into the prepared dish and place in a deep baking tray. Add boiling water to the tray until it reaches halfway up the side of the bowl and gently place in the oven. Cook for 45 minutes, or until the pudding is firm when touched. Let it sit for 5 minutes before serving.

 note

This recipe will work if you double the quantities, but add only 2 cups milk (not 2½ cups).

Quick berry trifles

2 cups mixed berries, reserving
  any juices

2 tablespoons caster sugar

2 cups pouring cream

1 teaspoon natural vanilla extract

250 g packet sponge finger biscuits

1 cup decaffeinated coffee

Preparation time: 20 minutes
Fridge time: 4 hours
Makes 6

This is a great dinner party dessert – make it the night before and let the flavours mature.

Strain the berries over a bowl to catch any juices. Gently combine the berries and half the sugar in a bowl. Whip the cream in a separate bowl with the vanilla and remaining sugar.

Combine the reserved berry juice and decaffeinated coffee in a wide bowl. Dip 2–3 sponge finger biscuits on both sides into the coffee mixture, break them into pieces and use them to layer the bases of 6 large serving glasses.

Add a dollop of cream to the biscuit layer, then a scattering of the berries. Repeat this process, finishing with a layer of cream. Chill the desserts in the refrigerator for at least 4 hours before serving.

✳ note

For a more adult version of this dessert, soak the biscuits in a combination of strong coffee and brandy, or your favourite liqueur, rather than the berry juice. For a little extra decadence, sprinkle with some finely grated good-quality dark chocolate just before serving.

STRAWBERRIES

Who doesn't love strawberries? Once you've grown your own fruit, with a flavour so sweet and mouth tingly, it will be hard to go back to bland store-bought ones. Like tomatoes, supermarket strawberries often look perfect but they lack the punch of the ones you grow yourself. Better still, if you grow your own you can be certain about what chemicals (if any) are used on the fruit.

How many strawberry plants should you have for a family? As many as you have room for, but we recommend at least six. If space is tight on the ground, use hanging baskets or any other pots you have lying around. As kids are so keen on strawberries, it's a great plant to get them interested in gardening. You could even make them responsible for their own little strawberry patch. The discipline of checking for weeds, pests and regular watering reinforces confidence and responsibility. Planting seedlings and waiting for them to grow into vegetables ready for harvest teaches them to be both accurate and patient. It also shows them that food doesn't come from a plastic bag.

Soil and site

You really need to set the soil up properly for a decent crop of strawberries. They need the soil to be ultra-rich in organic matter, like compost, manure, seaweed solution or a spread of blood and bone. Feed the soil well and build it into rows or mounds that are elevated about 10 cm above the rest of the bed, so the plants are well drained. Strawberries also need the sun to ripen properly, so if you are growing them in pots, make sure they exposed to full sun.

Planting

Plant strawberries in autumn in warm areas and in winter to spring in cool-climate areas. Strawberries are prone to viruses, so rather than pull runners from someone's garden, it is much better to buy virus-free plants from your local nursery.

Strawberries can be a tricky crop to grow from seed, so to save on any angst, we recommend that you just buy seedlings and go from there. Seedlings should be planted at least 30 cm apart to allow plenty of room for the plants to spread.

You can plant strawberries in barrels, hanging baskets and specialist strawberry pots. Some people also plant strawberries in hollowed out straw bales, which are filled with soil. This gives the strawberries a nutrient-rich and well-incubated bed.

Strawberry plants can get straggly in the off-seasons and generally last for two seasons before they need ripping out and starting again.

Growing

Strawberries need water. In hot weather, make sure you water every other day. Check pots to ensure they do not dry out as the flowers won't set if the plants are struggling. You can plant some other water-hungry plants such as lettuces and spinach nearby so you get the maximum use out of all this watering.

We also grow the herb borage among our strawberries. Borage can get wild and unwieldy, so you'll need to chop it back. However, the delicate flowers draw the bees into the garden bed and borage helps make the strawberries taste even sweeter. The blue flowers of borage make a pretty contrast to the red of the berries and green of the foliage, and the flowers can be used as a lovely garnish for summer garden salads and fruit salads, or can even be frozen in ice cubes.

Avoid planting any of the *brassicas* near strawberries. Both are heavy feeders and they will fail to thrive in the same pots or beds.

To improve the yield for an autumn crop of strawberries, prune the leaves back to about 2–3 cm of the crown and give the root zone a good feed with a complete fertiliser or seaweed solution. Once the flowers are setting into fruit, cover the soil with a layer of hay (or pine needles) for the berries to sit on so the fruit does not get wet and rot due to constantly touching the wet soil.

Harvesting

Strawberries are a summer crop but you may have a second harvest in autumn if you tend the plant well. Make sure you chop the plants right back again, to about 2–3 cm, after harvesting is complete. It will mean you have stronger plants the following season.

We recommend replacing the plants every two to three years to keep them vigorous.

Strawberries are best eaten the day they are picked, but if you have a glut they can be easily stewed or made into Stawberry Jam (page 187).

Pests

By far the biggest danger to the strawberry crop is children! In our experience, they sneak and eat the fruit off the runners the moment they see them. This is the crucial reason to make sure you don't use nasty chemicals on the crops. It's gorgeous to eat warm berries straight off the vine, but it is important kids know that some should make it to the table for a special sweet treat. Put children in charge of the picking – but watch them!

Birds also love to get at the ripe berries. It may be useful to net the plants, keeping the birds (and children) out. A simple net can be constructed making a tunnel from plastic piping and standard netting from the nursery.

We also like to edge our strawberry patch with the herbs pyrethrum and sage because they help to keep the insects at bay.

Quick ways with strawberries

- Drizzle with balsamic vinegar and serve with natural yoghurt or ice cream. Garnish using freshly chopped mint leaves.
- Add to cakes, muffins and puddings.
- Add to smoothies and milkshakes.
- Use as a topping on pancakes.

Strawberries in syrup

2 cups strawberries, hulled
   and large ones halved
juice of ½ lemon
2 tablespoons sugar

Preparation time: 5 minutes
Cooking time: 10 minutes
Serves 6

This sweet treat can be made well ahead of dinner and reheated when needed. This dish will keep for at least five days in an airtight container in the refrigerator, so you can treat yourself for a week.

Put the strawberries, lemon juice, sugar and ⅓ cup water in a saucepan and simmer slowly, without boiling, over medium–low heat for about 10 minutes, or until strawberries have softened and collapsed a little.

Serve the strawberries warm or chilled. For a quick weeknight dessert, spoon over some plain yoghurt or vanilla ice cream.

 notes

There are many ways you can serve this strawberry dessert. Buy some mini meringues (or make your own), whip some cream with vanilla extract and caster sugar and serve the meringues in a pretty bowl with the whipped cream and strawberries in syrup.

Alternatively, make some pikelets or pancakes and top with the strawberries in syrup and a dollop of Greek-style yoghurt.

Golden syrup dumplings

40 g unsalted butter, at
   room temperature

2 cups self-raising flour

2½ tablespoons milk

2 eggs

finely grated zest of 1 lemon

pinch of salt

SYRUP

juice of 1 lemon

1½ cups soft brown sugar

⅓ cup golden syrup

40 g unsalted butter

Preparation time: 20 minutes
Cooking time: 25 minutes
Serves 6–8

This is one of the most tempting winter desserts. It evokes childhood memories of puddings, pajamas and fireplaces. Serve the dumplings with ample syrup and thick cream or vanilla ice cream – or both! It is rich and filling and doesn't need any other adornments.

Combine the syrup ingredients with 2 cups water in a large, heavy-based saucepan over medium–high heat and simmer for 10–15 minutes, or until thickened and syrupy. Turn off the heat and leave in the saucepan until the dumpling mixture is ready.

To make the dumplings, use your fingers to work the butter into the flour in a large bowl so it looks like breadcrumbs. Make a well in the centre of the flour mixture. Lightly whisk the milk and eggs in a separate bowl and pour into the well. Add the lemon zest and salt and gently combine with a wooden spoon until it forms a dough-like consistency. Dust your hands with flour and roll all the dough into about 12 walnut-sized balls. Don't overwork the dough or it will become tough and rubbery.

Bring the syrup back to simmering point and place all the balls in. Reduce the heat to low, cover with a lid and cook for 10 minutes, or until the dumplings have doubled in size, gently turning during cooking so the dumplings are evenly coated in the syrup. Serve the dumplings with the syrup drizzled over the top.

✳ note

Prepare the syrup and dumplings separately earlier in they day if you want a quick and easy dessert that night. This is particularly handy when you have guests for dinner. These dumplings also taste fabulous recycled the next day – that is, if you have any leftovers!

S. O. S. Desserts

Store-bought piklets with jam and cream

Yoghurt, honey and fruit

Sliced apple and cheese (or sultanas and cheese)

Cinnamon toast

Banana split

Store-bought meringues, cream and
fresh berries

Fruit Salad

Baked stonefruit halves

Stewed (preserved fruit and custard
or yoghurt

Muesli Sundae

Baked lemon and rosewater cheesecake

200 g gingernut biscuits

40 g unsalted butter, melted

1 kg cream cheese

240 g caster sugar

3 tablespoons lemon juice

grated zest of 1 lemon

1 teaspoon natural vanilla extract
or the seeds of 2 vanilla beans

2 teaspoons rosewater (optional)

4 eggs, at room temperature

Preparation time: 20 minutes
Cooking time: 1 hour 40 minutes
Fridge time: 4 hours
Serves 8–10

A baked cheesecake is perfect for entertaining as you can make it a day ahead. Both little kids and big kids will love this one.

Preheat the oven to 170°C. Grease a round 23 cm spring-form tin. Place the tin on a large sheet of foil and press it up the outsides of the tin to seal. Repeat the process so it is double-wrapped.

Place the biscuits and melted butter in a food processor and pulse until finely ground. Spoon the biscuit mix into the base of the tin and press to form an even layer. Bake for 8–10 minutes, or until golden and fragrant. Set aside to cool.

Blend the cream cheese in a clean food processor until smooth. Add the sugar, lemon juice and zest, vanilla and rosewater and blend until combined. Add the eggs, one at a time, while the processor is still going.

Pour the mixture into the prepared tin. Place the tin in a deep baking tray on top of a cake cooling rack and pour in enough hot water to come about 2.5 cm up the side of the tin. Bake for 1–1½ hours, or until the top of the cake is golden brown and a skewer inserted comes out clean. Remove from the oven and take the tin out of the water removing the tinfoil immediately. Allow the cheesecake to cool completely in the tin. This will stop the base from going soggy. Carefully remove the cheesecake, lightly wrap in cling-wrap and refrigerate for at least 4 hours before serving. If desired, serve with cream and fresh berries or Easy Baked Rhubarb (page 177).

 note

To make a blueberry cheesecake fold 1½ cups blueberries through the cream cheese mixture once you have finished blending in the food processor. To make a strawberry cheesecake fold through 1½ cups hulled and quartered strawberries.

RHUBARB

Rhubarb is a long-term commitment for a gardener, but believe us, it's worth it. You'll need to find a permanent spot in a garden bed, at least 1 metre square, with plenty of sun and you'll need to feed it regularly. One vigorous healthy plant is enough to give a family a couple of crumbles and some stewed fruit for the breakfast cereal. However, we love it so much we need to have about four plants to make desserts and muffins, and to have enough stewed fruit for winter treats.

Rhubarb has a slightly tart, bitter flavour. But rather than loading rhubarb dishes and preserves with lots of sugar to tone down its tartness, we tend to stew the fruit with juice or cook it alongside other fruit, such as apples, to adjust its flavour. Rhubarb is a mild laxative and astringent, so it's good to serve to little ones if they have a bit of a tummy ache. Rhubarb is also good for the liver, so it makes a great dish for boozy dinner parties when the liver could do with an extra hand!

Beware – the leaves of rhubarb are poisonous. You'll need to keep kids away from handling the plant's leaves and dispose of the toxic greens immediately once you've harvested the rhubarb. Needless to say, avoid feeding the leaves to the chickens.

Soil and site

As with all plants, the soil is the key for growing rhubarb. Feed the soil before planting with ultra-rich organic matter, such as compost, manure, seaweed solution or even better, a spread of blood and bone.

Rhubarb will adapt well to most soil types, but the roots like to go deep, so make sure the organic matter is under the plant as well as scattered on top like a loose mulch. If the soil is mostly clay, plant the rhubarb on mounds to ensure drainage. Rhubarb also needs the sun to ripen properly, so avoid planting the fruit in shade.

Planting

Rhubarb is a cool-climate plant that thrives at around 10°C. It struggles in the heat – anything over about 25°C. Plant in late winter through to early summer, avoiding the peak of summer.

Rhubarb is best grown from the crown or as seedlings with a few stems present. Add plenty of manure or a complete fertiliser when planting rhubarb and make sure you water the plant well.

Growing

Rhubarb may struggle after planting as it hates transplants. For the best chance at keeping a healthy plant, make sure it is kept moist and mulched well.

Mulch and fertilise the plant regularly. We have a friend who planted a leftover fish head and carcass from dinner under a rhubarb plant. The plant has since thrived and looks stronger and more vibrant than ever. Failing fish dinner scraps, regular doses of seaweed solution would be just fine.

Cut back any flowers you see developing as you do not want rhubarb to go to seed. Also cut away any dead, or yellowing leaves. Flowers are a sign your plants are struggling – they need more food or water.

Pests

Plant sage and pyrethrum around the borders of the vegetable patches to help keep the insects away. Marigolds and nasturtiums also fill the gaps with colourful flowers and help keep the aphids and other nasty insects away from rhubarb.

You need to prevent the plant developing powdery mildew on the stalks or leaves. Make sure you plant rhubarb in well-drained soil, and mulch well so the stalks are not in contact with constantly wet soil.

Harvesting

You'll need to wait 12–18 months before you can harvest rhubarb. Summer and autumn are the key seasons for harvesting. Tend the plant carefully and you'll be able to encourage a healthy 'cut and come again' regime for the growing season.

Once the stems are starting to struggle to re-grow, cut them all off at the base of the plant, cover with manure and compost and water well. Allow the plant to lie dormant over winter and its stems will be all the more vigorous when they bounce back.

Quick ways with rhubarb

- Stew and spoon over plain yoghurt or cereal.

- Stew and stir through cereal or muesli.

- Pair with apple in a crumble.

- Finely chop and bake in muffins or cupcakes
  with apple and cinnamon.

- Combine with chopped strawberries and bake
  in pastry shells or brandy baskets.

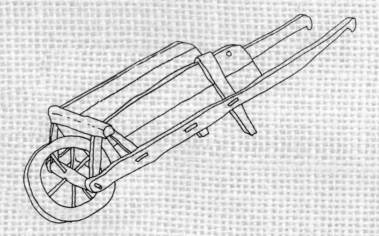

Easy baked rhubarb

5 rhubarb stalks, cut into
  2 cm lengths
1 cup orange juice
½ cup soft brown sugar

Preparation time: 5 minutes
Cooking time: 30 minutes
Makes 2 cups

This dish qualifies as an SOS dessert. Chop the rhubarb and whack it in the oven for a simple, delicious dessert.

Preheat the oven to 160°C. Spread the rhubarb in an even layer over the base of a 20 x 15 cm ovenproof dish. Pour the orange juice into the baking dish so it is 1 cm deep in the dish. The juice should not cover the rhubarb, just provide a layer to keep it moist. Sprinkle the sugar over the top.

Cook for 20–30 minutes, or until the rhubarb is soft but retains its shape when you pick it up with tongs. Most of the orange juice will have been absorbed by the rhubarb, or evaporated. If the rhubarb still seems raw and hard, add a splash of juice to the dish to keep it moist while the rhubarb finishes baking. The rhubarb will keep in an airtight container for up to 3 days.

Serve with Greek-style yoghurt, vanilla ice cream or meringues.

 note

Stewing rhubarb is the easiest thing in the world. Chop into 3 cm pieces, throw in a saucepan with a few tablespoons of soft brown sugar and enough water to just cover the rhubarb. Cook over low heat until thick and mushy – too easy.

Banana and chocolate cake

250 g unsalted butter, softened

¾ cup soft brown sugar

2 eggs

1½ cups self-raising flour

1 teaspoon bicarbonate of soda

½ teaspoon salt

3 over-ripe bananas, mashed

150 ml sour cream

1 cup small milk chocolate buttons

icing sugar

Preparation time: 15 minutes
Cooking time: 45 minutes
Serves 8–10

This is a beautiful, moist cake that the kids will adore. It keeps for up to a week in an airtight container, so it's a great lunchbox option. It's also a great cake for friends when they drop over for tea and a chat.

Preheat the oven to 160°C. Grease a ring tin about 8 cm deep and 20 cm in diameter. Beat the butter and sugar with a wooden spoon or electric beaters until creamy. Add the eggs, one at a time, beating well between each addition. Add the flour, bicarbonate of soda and salt and combine well. Add the bananas, sour cream or cream and chocolate buttons and gently mix.

Pour into the prepared cake tin and bake for 40–45 minutes, or until the cake is firm to touch and a skewer inserted into the middle comes out clean.

Allow to cool slightly in the tin before inverting onto a plate and dusting with icing sugar. This cake is delicious served warm from the oven, but it will keep in an airtight container for up to 1 week or in the freezer for up to 1 month.

✳ notes

If you don't have a ring tin, you can use any other shape – loaf tins, round tins, and so on. If you change the size of the tin, cut down the cooking time by about 10 minutes and check to see if the skewer comes out clean.

If you prefer, make this cake in individual muffin trays (or cupcake bases) on a Sunday night for lunches throughout the week. Put into cupcake cases and bake for about 15 minutes.

French-style apple galettes

3 sheets butter puff pastry

6 granny smith apples (or any crisp, sour apple in season)

½ cup apricot or raspberry jam

Preparation time: 20 minutes
Cooking time: 10 minutes
Serves 6

These are simple, French-inspired tarts that can be served for a dinner party. Commercial puff pastry is so easy to work with; once you have tried this dessert you will be converted to the versatility of puff.

Preheat the oven to 180°C. Using a saucer, cut out six 13 cm circles from the pastry. Place the pastry rounds on baking trays.

Cut the apples into quarters, discard the core and thinly slice. Arrange the apple slices, slightly overlapping, in a fan-shape on top of the pastry rounds. Brush the tops of the apple slices with the jam. Put the galettes in the oven and cook for 10 minutes, or until golden on top.

 notes

This dish also works well with peaches. They need to be firm to the touch so that they can be easily cut without turning mushy. If you are lucky enough to have a tree, it's a great way to use a glut of peaches.

If cutting circles into the pastry seems too tricky, just use the square sheet of pastry as is. You can layer the apple slices in rows, and use a pizza knife to cut into serving portions.

Mimma's easy butter cake

125 g unsalted butter, softened
1 cup caster sugar
1 ½ cups plain flour
3 eggs
1 ½ teaspoons baking powder
1 teaspoon salt
½ cup milk
1 teaspoon natural vanilla extract

ICING
125 g unsalted butter, softened
1½ cups icing sugar
1½ tablespoons milk

Preparation time: 10 minutes
Cooking time: 40 minutes
Serves 6–8

This is a foolproof one-dish wonder from Kirsty's super-mum. We all use it for birthday cakes, afternoon teas or any occasion when we want to whip up a quick cake. You can double or triple the quantities with ease. The mixture also makes great cupcakes, just allow no more than 15 minutes in the oven. Left un-iced, the cake (or cupcakes) will last 3–4 days stored in an airtight container.

Preheat the oven to 180°C. Grease and line a 20 cm round tin (or tin shape of your choice). Combine all the ingredients in a bowl and, using an electric mixer, beat for 5 minutes, or until creamy and fluffy. Pour the cake mixture into the prepared tin. Bake for 30–40 minutes, or until a skewer inserted in the centre of the cake comes out clean. Allow the cake cool before icing.

To make the icing, beat the butter with electric beaters until pale and creamy. Gradually add the icing sugar. If the mixture needs more moisture, add milk, in small amounts, to create the desired consistency. When spreading the icing, use a knife dipped in boiling water.

✳ notes

You can vary the flavour of this cake by adding 1 cup sifted cocoa powder, 2 tablespoons grated lemon or orange zest, or 1 cup desiccated coconut.

To vary the flavour of the icing, add 2 tablespoons lemon or orange zest or 2 tablespoons sifted cocoa powder. For coloured icing, add a few drops of food colouring at a time and mix through until the selected colour is to your liking.

Apple and rhubarb betty

3 granny smith apples (or any crisp, sour apple in season), cored and roughly chopped

4 rhubarb stems, cut into 2 cm lengths

2 teaspoons ground cinnamon

½ whole nutmeg, freshly grated

1 cup plain flour

1 cup soft brown sugar

100 g unsalted butter, cut into small cubes

½ cup rolled oats

Preparation time: 15 minutes
Cooking time: 35 minutes
Serves 6

A 'betty' is simply a crumble with extra crumble in the middle – making it twice as delicious!

Preheat the oven to 180°C. Grease a 25 × 20 cm ovenproof baking dish. Combine the apple and rhubarb with half the cinnamon and nutmeg in a bowl and mix well. Spread half the fruit mixture into the base of the baking dish.

In a separate bowl, combine the flour and sugar with the remaining cinnamon and nutmeg and mix well. Add the butter cubes and use the tips of your fingers to pinch the butter into the flour mixture, so that it combines well and looks like fine breadcrumbs.

Spread half the flour mixture over the fruit mixture in the baking dish, then cover this layer with the remaining fruit mixture.

Add the rolled oats to the remaining flour mixture and combine well. Spread the flour and oat mixture over the top of the fruit mixture. Cover the dish with foil and bake for 25 minutes. Remove the foil and cook for a further 5–10 minutes, or until the top is golden and bubbling.

Nutty ice cream sundaes

8 scoops good-quality vanilla ice cream

⅓ cup toasted muesli

2 tablespoons lecithin or bran

2 tablespoons wheat germ

2 tablespoons honey

2 tablespoons nuts, such as crushed peanuts, chopped macadamias or slivered almonds

Preparation time: 10 minutes
Cooking time: none
Serves 4

This is one of those desserts that strikes a balance: it tastes great and is nutritious as well. Warm the honey for 10–15 seconds in the microwave and it will be much easier to pour.

Put 2 scoops of ice cream into bowls or glasses. Sprinkle with the muesli, lecithin and wheat germ. Drizzle with the honey and top with the crushed nuts.

Relishes, preserves and pickles

This chapter comprises the well-tested recipes of our mothers, mothers-in-law, grandmothers, great-grandmothers and friends. Our relatives sure knew how to make a little bit of food last a long time. We've included classics such as Strawberry Jam and Easy Marmalade, Pickled Onions and Bread and Butter Cucumbers. For something a little more exotic we've included an Indian-inspired Plum Chutney and a delicious Apricot Chutney.

Part of the magic of growing your own fruit and vegetables is extending the season. Many crops have a glut at the end of the season, which are perfect for preserving and pickling – green tomatoes make a wonderful chutney, tiny onions can be pickled, lemons can be preserved in salt.

Add a blast of sunshine and summer to your cereal by dishing up preserved berries in winter, or spread marmalade or jam on your toast. We even stir jam through porridge in winter or serve it with pikelets and cream for dessert.

You'll need time to make these recipes. Plan an afternoon get-together with some friends – communal cooking is the new bookclub. While adults have a glass of wine and chat the kids can play and help chop, stir and make colourful labels for the jars.

Don't throw your hands in the air if you don't have a garden. You can still make all the recipes here. Simply buy the ingredients from the markets, greengrocer or supermarket when they are cheap and in season. You can often get discounted tomatoes, plums and nectarines in boxes. Buy a box, grab a crowd, make a few batches and you can all take some home.

The recipes in this section require jars to be properly sterilised and sealed. Lower the jars and lids into a large saucepan of boiling water and simmer for 10 minutes, then remove and allow to dry completely. Alternatively, lay the jars on their sides in a 120°C oven for about 10 minutes before using. Once the preserve has set in the jars (leave covered with a clean cloth for about 8 hours), place the lids in boiling water, remove and screw firmly into place.

Strawberry jam

2 kg strawberries, hulled
juice of 4 lemons
1.5 kg white sugar

Preparation time: 10 minutes
Cooking time: 50 minutes
Makes about 1.5 litres

When making jam, generally the weight of the fruit is matched by the weight of the sugar. We've reduced the sugar level here because strawberries are already sweet, especially the ones you grow yourself.

Combine the strawberries and lemon juice in a saucepan over medium heat and simmer for 30–45 minutes, or until the berries are very soft.

Meanwhile, warm the sugar in a baking dish in a low-temperature oven until lukewarm. This helps the fruit and sugar to blend.

Add the sugar to the pan and simmer until the sugar has dissolved, then boil the mixture rapidly, stirring occasionally, for 20 minutes, or until it has reached setting point.

To check if the jam is ready, do a set test. Put a teaspoon of the jam mixture onto a small plate and place in the freezer for 1–2 minutes. If a skin has formed on the surface of the jam it is ready to bottle. Once this stage has been reached, take the pan off the heat and allow to cool for a few minutes.

Pour the mixture into sterilised jars (see page 186) and allow to cool. This jam will keep for at least a year.

 note

This recipe works well by replacing the same quantity of strawberries with raspberries, blackberries or gooseberries. Just reduce the amount of lemon juice to 2 teaspoons for blackberries or gooseberries as these berries have a higher acid and pectin content. The cooking time will vary depending on the fruit's softness, so make sure you always do a set test.

Easy marmalade

4 sweet oranges, finely diced
1 lemon, finely diced
2.2 litres boiling water
1.3 kg white sugar

Preparation time: 24 hours
Cooking time: 30 minutes
Makes about 1 litre

Every household should have a jar of marmalade on the shelf. It just seems to be the type of spread that visitors always request for their toast. Kids will happily eat it too – as long as it isn't too bitter.

This recipe is an easy one, handed-down from Kirsty's great-grandmother. Kirsty's mother Carolyn has also used it for years and it can be made in one small batch. Simply double or triple the quantities if you are lucky enough to have a surplus of oranges.

Put the orange and lemon slices in a large bowl and pour over the boiling water. Cover the bowl and leave overnight, or up to 24 hours.

Transfer the fruit and water to a large, heavy-based saucepan and bring to the boil over medium–high heat, reduce the heat and simmer for 20 minutes, or until the fruit is tender.

Meanwhile, warm the sugar in a baking dish in a low-temperature oven until lukewarm. This helps the fruit and sugar to blend.

Add the sugar to the pan and simmer until the sugar has dissolved, then boil the mixture rapidly, stirring occasionally, for 20 minutes, or until it has reached setting point.

To check if the marmalade is ready, do a set test. Put a teaspoon of the marmalade mixture onto a small plate and place in the freezer for 1–2 minutes. If a skin has formed on the surface of the marmalade it is ready to bottle. Once this stage has been reached, take the pan off the heat and allow to cool for a few minutes.

Pour the mixture into sterilised jars (see page 186) and allow to cool. This marmalade will keep for at least a year.

 note

Never make jam or marmalade with small children about as the temperature of boiling jam is very high. Also, you should always use a saucepan larger than the quantity of the jam mixture so that there is no chance it will boil over. Children can help by picking the fruit, washing the jars and decorating the labels.

Nana Deegan's apricot chutney

1 kg apricots, halved and stoned

4½ cups soft brown sugar

600 ml white or malt vinegar

3 white onions, diced

2 tablespoons salt

1 teaspoon mixed spice

1½ teaspoons ground ginger

2 teaspoons cayenne pepper

400 g sultanas

Preparation time: 15 minutes
Cooking time: 2½ hours
Makes about 1.5 litres

Kirsty's grandmother is the queen of chutney and this apricot recipe is sublime. We tend to make enough batches of this chutney to give away as Christmas presents – with labels decorated by the kids. This recipe is equally as delicious with nectarines instead of apricots.

Combine all the ingredients in a large, heavy-based saucepan and bring to the boil over high heat. Reduce the heat and simmer for 2½ hours, or until the mixture has reduced and thickened.

Pour the mixture into sterilised jars (see page 186) and allow to cool. This chutney will keep for at least a year.

Eunie's zucchini relish

1 kg zucchini, grated

2 tablespoons salt

1 onion, finely chopped

2 cups sugar

2 cups white vinegar

1 teaspoon mustard seeds

1 teaspoon curry powder

1 teaspoon ground turmeric

3 tablespoons plain flour

Preparation time: 15 minutes
Cooking time: 1½ hours
Makes about 1.5 litres

This is another grandmother special, given to us by a friend. Eunie was a whiz at relishes and preserves, and her daughter and granddaughter have inherited her love of cooking. This is a tangy soft relish that goes well with leftover meats and cheeses, making it perfect for sandwiches.

Put the zucchini in a large bowl, add the salt, cover with water and soak for 2 hours. Drain well then put the zucchini, onion, sugar, vinegar, mustard seeds, curry powder and ground turmeric in a heavy-based saucepan over low heat and simmer for 1 hour, stirring occasionally, until soft and slightly reduced. Remove the saucepan from the heat.

Mix the flour with ½ cup water to make a smooth paste. Stir the paste through the zucchini mixture and return the saucepan to high heat and bring to the boil. When the relish has hit boiling point, pour the mixture into sterilised jars (see page 186) and allow to cool. This relish will keep for 2–3 months.

Eunie's tomato relish

6 kg tomatoes, roughly chopped

2 kg onions, roughly chopped

2 large handfuls salt

2 cups brown vinegar

2 kg sugar

⅓ cup curry powder

3 tablespoons mustard seeds

1 teaspoon cayenne pepper

1 cup plain flour

Preparation time: 12 hours
Cooking time: 1 hour
Makes about 4 litres

Tomatoes are so exciting to grow that we often plant way more than we need. This is a fantastic recipe to use up all those tomatoes at the peak of the growing season. Keep the tomatoes and onions chunky, which will give you a lovely texture for the relish.

Put the tomato and onion in a bowl and stir through the salt. Cover and leave to stand overnight. Drain the excess juice from the bowl and transfer the tomato and onion mixture to a heavy-based saucepan over medium–high heat. Add the vinegar and sugar to the pan, bring to the boil and simmer for 1 hour, or until softened and the mixture has reduced and thickened.

Stir through the curry powder, mustard seeds and cayenne pepper. Mix the flour with ½ cup water to make a smooth paste. Stir the paste through the tomato relish mixture.

Pour the mixture into sterilised jars (see page 186) and allow to cool. This relish will keep for 2–3 months.

Barb's plum chutney

100 m olive oil

1 leek, thinly sliced

2 red onions, thinly sliced

1½ tablespoons ground cumin

1½ tablespoons ground coriander

1½ tablespoons curry powder

1 teaspoon ground cardamom

1 teaspoon smoked paprika

1 teaspoon garam masala

juice of 3 lemons

2 kg plums, chopped coarsely,
    stones discarded

1 cup brown vinegar

1 kg sugar

1 teaspoon salt

Preparation time: 30 minutes
Cooking time: 3 hours
Makes about 1.5 litres

Peta's mum Barb passed on this recipe when Kirsty brought over a huge bag of plums she had bought at a roadside stall. The 3 hour cooking time may seem excessive, but let this chutney slowly simmer away on an evening when you are curled up with a good book. Just remember to get up and stir the pan from time to time.

Heat the oil in a saucepan over medium heat and sauté the leek and onion for 3–4 minutes, or until softened. Remove from the heat and allow to cool. Combine the spices with the juice of 1 lemon to make a paste, then stir through the leek and onion mixture.

Put the plums, vinegar, sugar and remaining lemon juice in a heavy-based saucepan over low heat, stirring occasionally, until the sugar dissolves. Add the leek mixture and salt. Cook over low heat for 3 hours, until the mixture has reduced and thickened. Pour into sterilised jars (see page 186) and allow to cool. This chutney will keep for at least a year.

Tomato and sultana chutney

2 kg ripe tomatoes, diced

1.5 kg granny smith apples, diced

1 kg onion, diced

1 kg sugar

250 g sultanas

6 garlic cloves

½ teaspoon cayenne pepper

1 litre brown vinegar

2 tablespoons salt

1 tablespoon cloves

1 tablespoon ground white pepper

Preparation time: 15 minutes
Cooking time: 5 hours
Makes about 2 litres

This chutney takes 5 hours to cook, so we recommend that you get a crew together for the afternoon, have a glass of wine and make a couple of other relishes and chutneys too. This way, everyone can go home with a few jars of preserves to see out the year.

Combine all the ingredients in a large, heavy-based saucepan over high heat. Bring to the boil, reduce the heat and simmer for 5 hours, until the mixture has reduced and thickened. Pour into sterilised jars (see page 186) and allow to cool. This chutney will keep for at least a year.

ONIONS

Onion, combined with its cousin garlic, forms the foundation of so many of the dishes in any household: curries, soups, stocks, sauces, savoury tarts – the list is endless.

Although onions have none of the instant attraction for children as strawberries, tomatoes and sweet corn, kids will love digging them up. Besides, as the starting point for so many family meals we think it is important to try to grow at least a few.

If you successfully grow onions, have a go at growing a few more the following year. Soon enough, you be growing white, brown and red onions, plus planting enough so you can pull the young ones up as spring onions for tasty salads. If you feel like treating yourself, why not just plant the French favourite: shallots. These are the tiny brown onions that are packed full of flavour and bring depth to any dish. Your soups will never be quite the same again.

Soil and site

Onions don't tend to thrive in freshly prepared manured and composted soils. Instead, plant them in soils that have been undisturbed for a few months. If you give onions the perfectly rich soil you need for the *brassicas*, the green stems and shoots will flourish. However, we want the bulb below the ground to grow, not the greenery. So, the soil needs to be rich and well-drained – just not too rich.

Onions need plenty of sun, so make sure they are planted in full sun. Crop rotation is also important for onions – plant them following a crop of silverbeet, cabbage or lettuce.

Planting

Plant onions while the weather is cool: autumn, winter and early spring. Traditionally the prime planting time for onion seeds is the winter solstice. There are varieties to go with each season (early, mid and late) so check the seed packets carefully to ensure you plant at the right time.

We advise planting onions as seeds straight into the ground as it's easy to damage the roots and baby bulb base when you transplant seedlings. It takes over two weeks for the seeds to germinate, so be patient. Alternatively, you can buy seedlings. Plant seedlings out when they are 5 mm thick. Space them about 10 cm apart and 3 cm deep.

We suggest a continuous planting of onions every month through the growing season. Have a think about the number of bags of onions your family consumes every month and it suddenly becomes plausible that you can have enough to last through the year.

Growing

For spring onions, sew plants every four weeks and harvest when they are small. You can also get particular spring onion varieties – just ask your local nursery to recommend some.

Onions can prevent apple scab on apple trees, so it pays to plant a large selection of onions under apple trees if you have any.

Be vigilant about watering onions – too much watering and poorly drained soil can rot the bulb and lead to mildew on the green stem.

Pests

The main pest for onions is onion fly. Alternate rows, or squares, of onions with carrots and parsley as they help to deter this pest.

Harvesting

Traditionally, the best time to harvest onions is the summer solstice (the longest day of the year). However, harvesting will depend on the variety and time you planted the onion.

To get the smaller onions for pickling, ask your local nursery for a smaller variety, or dig up the onions when they are about half the size of a golf ball. Full-sized onions should be harvested only when their green foliage turns yellow and starts to die off. Get the kids to help you, and do it slowly, with a hand-fork or trowel to avoid chopping any onions in half.

Once you have harvested the onions, lay them on racks to air in the sun to dry out. Avoid getting them wet at all costs. Chop the tops off, or use them to string the onions together. Store onions in a cool, dark place until ready for use.

Quick ways with onions

- Dice and combine with garlic to form the foundation of curries, stews, casseroles, stir-fries, soups and stocks.
- Red onions and spring onions are superb in salads and as a fresh garnish on seafood and Asian-inspired dishes.
- Combine with fresh herbs and ripe tomatoes to make a Mexican-style salsa.
- Add to quiches and tarts.
- Use as pickles and relishes.

Pickled onions

2 kg pickling onions, peeled

1 tablespoon salt

2.25 litres malt vinegar

250 g sugar

PICKLING SPICES

2 teaspoons peeled and chopped
   fresh ginger or 1 teaspoon
   ground ginger

2 teaspoons minced garlic

2 teaspoons peppercorns

1 teaspoon allspice

1 teaspoon cloves

1 teaspoon mustard seeds

1 teaspoon nutmeg

1 teaspoon salt

3 bay leaves (or 1 for each jar
   of onions)

2–3 small red chillies (or 1 for
   each jar of onions)

Preparation time: 24 hours
Cooking time: 10 minutes
Makes 2.5 litres

Keep a jar of pickled onions on the shelf and you'll have a ready-made treat to pack into a picnic hamper or pop in a lunchbox with a Mini Ploughman's Lunch (see page 19).

Cover the onions with water and the salt in a container and stand overnight. Drain the brine and pack the onions tightly into sterilised jars (see page 186).

Bring the vinegar, sugar and pickling spices to the boil over high heat, stirring occasionally, for 5 minutes. Remove from the heat and fill the jars with the hot vinegar mixture. Allow the mixture to cool and seal the jars. Store the onions for at least 2 weeks to enhance the flavours before eating. These pickled onions will last for 2–3 months.

note

If you don't have the time to make your own, pickling spice mixes can be purchased at most large supermarkets.

Green tomato pickles

1.5 kg green tomatoes, diced
1.5 kg onions, diced
1 cup salt
6 large garlic cloves, crushed
200 g seedless raisins
4 cups vinegar
1.5 kg soft brown or raw sugar
1 cup plain flour
2 teaspoons cayenne pepper
1 tablespoon ground ginger

Preparation time: 24 hours
Cooking time: 30 minutes
Makes about 2 litres

There always seems to be a glut of green tomatoes at the end of every summer – which is why we created this pickle recipe. These tomato pickles go particularly well with quiche, cheese or cold cuts of meat, and make a delicious addition to most sandwiches. If you're using cherry tomatoes, keep them whole and add an extra 15 minutes to the cooking time.

Combine the tomato and onion in a bowl, stir through the salt and cover with water. Cover and allow to stand overnight.

Drain well then put the tomato and onion, garlic and raisins in a heavy-based saucepan over medium–high heat and simmer for 20 minutes, stirring occasionally, until well softened.

Meanwhile, combine the vinegar, sugar, flour and spices in a large bowl and add to the tomato mixture. Bring the mixture back to the boil and simmer for a further 5 minutes. Pour into sterilised jars (see page 186) and allow to cool. These pickles will last for 2–3 months.

Sue's zucchini pickles

1.5 kg zucchini, thinly sliced
2 small onions, thinly sliced
1 small red capsicum, thinly sliced
3 tablespoons salt
2 cups white vinegar
2 cups sugar
1 teaspoon celery seeds
1 teaspoon ground turmeric
2 teaspoons mustard seeds

Preparation time: 2 hours
Cooking time: 2 ¼ hours
Makes about 1.5 litres

Sue Wilcox – Kirsty's mother-in-law – always seems to have a jar or two of zucchini pickles lurking in her cupboard. Sue whips them out for an impromptu picnic, a lunch of cold cuts or to spice up a simple lunch of bread and cheese.

Combine the zucchini, onion and capsicum in a large bowl, stir through the salt and cover with water. Cover and stand for 2 hours.

Drain the excess juice from the bowl. Heat the remaining ingredients in a large, heavy-based saucepan and bring to the boil over medium–high heat, stirring, until the sugar dissolves. Pour this mixture over the drained vegetables, stir through and stand for 2 hours.

Return this mixture back to the pan and bring to the boil for 5 minutes. Pour into sterilised jars (see page 186) and allow to cool. These pickles will last for 2–3 months.

CUCUMBERS

Cucumbers are one of those fantastically versatile vegetables that can jazz up a meal or salad in minutes. When the weather is hot, the humble cucumber can be used as a face mask, a healthy snack or to bulk up a garden salad. You can even add a few slices to freshen up a fruit punch or the classic summer drink, Pimms and ginger ale.

The so-called burpless cucumber varieties generally make better eating. The rounder apple-style cucumbers with a white skin are great for a novelty factor. If you're planning on bottling cucumbers, you'll need to grow the tiny pickling varieties, as the skins are tougher and they last much longer.

Soil and site
Make sure your soil is fertile before planting cucumbers by adding manure and compost, or a complete fertiliser six weeks before planting. The soil will also need to be well-drained. Cucumbers like partial shade, so protect them from the full blast of hot sun.

Planting
Cucumbers are a warm-weather crop. The growing season is short, so plant mid-spring to early summer. Don't plant until the frosts have finished for at least a month. Frosts will damage, or even kill, the plants.

Cucumbers have sensitive root systems, so we generally prefer to plant the seedlings purchased from a nursery. Plant cucumber seedlings in 5 cm deep circular divots about 30 cm across. By planting the cucumbers in shallow holes, you can catch the water and protect the roots of the plant. Plant two seedlings in each hole and prune to the ground the one that fails to thrive. This way you can be sure to grow the strongest plant.

Growing
Cucumbers are a high-maintenance plant. As cucumbers are mostly comprised of water, they'll need plenty of it to grow. You will notice on hot days that the plants will quickly wilt, so keep the water supply up. If you're growing cucumbers in pots, don't let the soil dry out. Fertilise the plants with a seaweed solution or a complete fertiliser about a fortnight after planting.

To aid the pollination of flowers, make sure you have plenty of companion plants with blue flowers to draw the bees to your vegetable patch. This includes catmint, sage, lavender, borage and cornflower. Grow cucumbers under peas and beans for nutrients and sunflowers and sweet corn for shade. Cucumbers also like being companion planted with potatoes, celery and lettuce.

Pests
Aphids are cucumbers' main pest, but they can be avoided by ensuring the beds and pots are companion planted with orange-coloured nasturtiums. A border of sage and pyrethrum will also deter insects from your vegetable patch.

The cucumber beetle is a potential problem, but they don't like radishes, so plant some radish seeds continuously while the cucumbers are in season.

Cucumber leaves and fruit can get a bit mildewy, so mulch the beds well so the fruit sits on straw, rather than wet soil. Also, avoid watering the leaves overhead – water the root zone only.

Harvesting
Cucumbers will be ready to harvest within three months of planting. You'll need to harvest them as soon as they are ripe, or slightly immature. They quickly go soft and squishy if you leave them on the plant. Large cucumbers can be kept in the fridge for up to one week, but the smaller ones will need to be pickled immediately.

Quick ways with cucumbers
- Combine in a blender with plain yoghurt, garlic and lemon juice as a dip, with sliced cucumbers, carrots and celery on the side.
- Finely dice and serve with yoghurt as a side dish to cool down Indian dishes and curries.
- Slice and add to sandwiches, roll-ups and salads.
- Slice and place on your face and eyes for a refreshing pick-me-up while you lie down for 10 minutes.

Bread and butter cucumbers

4 large cucumbers, thinly sliced
salt
2 cups white vinegar
¾ cup sugar
2 teaspoons mustard seeds
½ small red capsicum, thinly sliced

Preparation time: 30 minutes
Cooking time: 20 minutes
Makes about 1.5 litres

This cucumber recipe has been a staple of Kirsty's mother-in-law, Sue, for decades. Fresh cucumbers tend to go soggy quickly, so this is a good way of using up a glut of the crisp vegies from your garden. As the name suggests, these are great in sandwiches, with cold meat and cheese.

Arrange the cucumber slices in layers in a large shallow dish, sprinkling a little salt between each layer. Cover and stand overnight.

Rinse the cucumber thoroughly under cold water and drain well. Combine the vinegar, sugar, mustard seeds, 1 teaspoon salt and 1 cup water in a saucepan and bring to the boil over high heat, stirring until the sugar dissolves. Reduce heat and simmer, uncovered, for 5 minutes. Add the cucumber to the pan, bring back to the boil, then remove from the heat.

While still hot, pack the cucumber tightly into sterilised jars (see page 186), adding a few thin strips of red capsicum. Fill with the vinegar mixture and seal when cold. These bread and butter cucumbers will keep for 2–3 months.

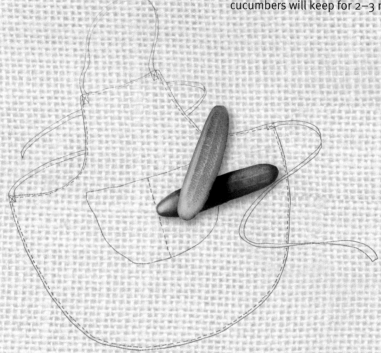

Preserved lemons

lemons, as many to fit the jars
  you have

rock salt, at least 1 teaspoon
  per lemon

whole cloves, 2–3 per jar

whole peppercorns, 2–3 per jar

bay leaves, 1 per jar

cinnamon sticks, 1 per jar

Preparation time: 10 minutes
Cooking time: none
Makes as many jars as you wish

Preserved lemons add a distinctive Middle Eastern zing to a whole range of dishes. Stuff the rind under the skin of a chicken before roasting or into a rolled shoulder of lamb, or dice finely and add to Greek-style yoghurt with a drizzle of honey. With a can of lentils, preserved lemon, parsley, salt and pepper, you'll never want for an instant salad again.

Just remember the rind is the tastiest bit, and you'll need to wash the salty brine away before you use the skin.

Quarter the lemons lengthways, leaving them joined at the base. Smother the flesh of the lemons with rock salt (use at least 1 teaspoon per lemon). Pack the lemons tightly inside sterilised jars (see page 186), covering with additional rock salt.

Add 2–3 cloves, 2–3 peppercorns, 1 bay leaf and 1 cinnamon stick to each jar. Top the jar with rock salt – this sucks the moisture out of the lemons and preserves them. Top the jar with lemon juice to remove any air from the jar and seal. Leave for at least 2 months before using. Preserved lemons will last at room temperature for up to 6 months.

 note

If you spot a box of limes in season, or you are lucky enough to have a fruiting lime tree, then you can also make preserved limes following this recipe. Or, for a more citrus twist, add lemon leaves or kaffir lime leaves to the jars of preserved lemon.

Stewed fruit

500 g fruit

1–2 tablespoons sugar (depending on the sourness or acid level of the fruit – test for sweetness)

Preparation time: 10 minutes
Cooking time: 10 minutes
Makes about 500 g

It's so easy and inexpensive to stew up 500 g batches of whatever fruit is in season. The flavour of many fruits, such as apples and apricots, become richer and sweeter when cooked. In summer, look for cherries, berries, plums, peaches, apricots and nectarines. In autumn and winter, look out for pears, apples and rhubarb.

If you can't be bothered collecting and sterilising jars, then this is the perfect recipe for you, as stewed fruit can be made then packed into old yoghurt or ice cream containers – whatever is handy. This way, you can have treats stored in the freezer right throughout the year.

If you are using apples and pears: peel, quarter, core and slice the fruit. If you are using soft stone fruit such as apricots, nectarines, plums or cherries: halve them and remove the stones (or leave them whole if you prefer).

To make the syrup, combine the sugar and 1 cup water in a saucepan over medium heat, stirring until the sugar dissolves. Increase the heat and bring to the boil for 3 minutes. (Watch closely as sugar can boil over the top of saucepans easily.)

Reduce the heat, add the fruit to the syrup and simmer for about 10 minutes, or until the fruit is tender but retains its shape. Once cooked, stewed fruit should be kept in the refrigerator and used within a few days. Large quantities may be packed into containers or freezer bags and stored in the freezer for up to 3 months.

Bottled fruit

½ cup sugar
1 kg fruit
2 cups water

Preparation time: 20 minutes
Cooking time: 25 minutes
Makes about 1 kg

There's something comforting about a shelf lined with jars of fruit – it always manages to feel like home. As a little girl, Kirsty remembers her mother Carolyn preserving fruit each summer. This was partly because it was cheapest to buy fruit in bulk when it was in-season and partly because they lived on a farm a long way from anywhere – there was no dashing down the road for treats. Preserved fruit meant they had fruit on hand throughout the year.

Carolyn's own mother used to preserve fruit and the tradition has passed from mother to daughter – as with so many families. Across generations and landscapes, jars full of pretty coloured fruit line the pantry shelves every year.

Bottled fruit is also a healthy alternative to sugary treats. The sterilisation process, rather than the added sugar, preserves the fruit – so, if you like, the fruit may be bottled without any additional sugar.

To make the syrup, heat the sugar and 2 cups water in a saucepan over medium heat, stirring until the sugar dissolves. Increase the heat and bring to the boil for 3 minutes. (Watch closely as sugar can boil over the top of saucepans easily.) Allow the syrup to cool to room temperature before pouring into jars.

Pack the fruit tightly into sterilised jars (see page 186) then fill with the cooled syrup. Seal the jars tightly.

Line the base of a large, deep saucepan with cardboard or a thick tea towel and place the filled jars on top. Fill the saucepan with cold water to come about two-thirds up the sides of the jars.

Bring to the boil over medium–high heat and simmer for 25 minutes. (It must be at least 25 minutes, so the fruit is fully sterilised.) Remove the pan from the heat and allow to cool.

Remove the jars from the saucepan and leave, untouched, for at least 12 hours. Ensure that the jars are firmly sealed before storing in a cool, dry place. Refrigerate once the jars have been opened.

 note

There are a number of suitable jars for preserving fruit, but all must have tight-fitting lids with rubber rings to create an airtight seal. Some jars need spring-loaded clips to hold the lid in position during processing. The clips and jars can be reused year after year. Stainless steel lids are more expensive to purchase, but last much longer than other metal lids. Rubber rings need to be replaced with each use.

Index

Thank you

To our publishing team at Hardie Grant – Sandy Grant, Julie Pinkham, Mary Small and Fran Berry – thanks for being so supportive of the concept from the outset. Thanks also to the best illustrated book editor in the business, Ellie Smith, for her enthusiasm, frankness, encouragement and discerning eye. Thanks to Paul McNally, copyeditor and project manager extraordinaire and Trisha Garner for the beautiful design. The detail and finesse from both have made this book very special.

Thank you to the team who put together a fabulous and fun food shoot in the studio: stylist Deb Kaloper, photography assistant (and budding food critic!) Christine Francis and editor Jane Winning for all her work behind the scenes.

We must also acknowledge Lana Philips, horticulturalist with the Ian Potter Foundation Children's Garden at the Royal Botanic Gardens, Melbourne. Lana read multiple versions of the gardening parts of the manuscript and gave valuable technical feedback for growing vegetables for children and families. We are very grateful for her enthusiasm and time.

Thanks to all our friends and family who tested recipes, and in many cases, provided us with some of their own favourites. In particular we'd like to acknowledge: Kate Heine (page 11), John Heitman (page 13), Sue Wilcox (pages 32, 197, 198, 202, 206–207), Lisa Phillipe (page 78), Richard Manning (page 124), Carolyn Manning (pages 182, 188, 206–207), Brenda Deegan (pages 187, 190, 193), Vicky Hawken (pages 190, 191, 198) and Barb Heine (page 193).

Thanks to Fiona Laird and her daughter Julia Barrett (pages ix, 119, 172) for being good sports during various photo shoots and, indeed, throughout the entire production of this book!

We are very grateful to Vicky Hawken and Barb Heine for allowing us to take the occasional shot in their vegie patches when Kirsty's crops were out of season or decimated by bugs!

Kirsty would like to thank her parents, Richard and Carolyn Manning and sister, Pru Hannon, for their love and support over the years. Part of Kirsty's inspiration for this book stemmed from the loving family life and great food she had growing up. Super in-laws John and Sue Wilcox have also been a tremendous support.

Peta would like to thank and express her love for her daughters, Issy and Charlotte Penny, for teaching her humility and hilarity and her brother Marc for his love and food talk. She would also like to thank her sister Kate for everything that words cannot express.

Lastly, our love and gratitude to Jacqui Henshaw – photographer, artist and now great friend – who not only has a beautiful eye, but a beautiful heart. May we have many more special projects together!

Published in 2010 by
Hardie Grant Books
85 High Street
Prahran, Victoria 3181, Australia
www.hardiegrant.com.au

Published in the United Kingdom in
2010 by Hardie Grant Books (London)

Cataloguing-in-Publication data is available from the National Library of Australia.

ISBN 978 1 74066 696 1

Edited by Paul McNally
Design by Trisha Garner
Photography by Jacqui Henshaw
Styling by Deborah Kaloper
Indexing by Lucy Malouf
Handwritten notes by Deborah Reidy
Colour reproduction by Splitting Image Colour Studio
Printed and bound in China by
C & C Offset Printing

10 9 8 7 6 5 4 3 2 1

The publisher would like to thank the following for their generosity in supplying props for the book: Empire Vintage, Frances Roberts at Marmalade Café, Izzi & Popo, Made in Japan, Market Import, Moss, Warehouse 8 and Wilkins and Kent.